Fear and Trembling in Las Vegas

Fear and Trembling in Las Vegas

An Unintended Journey to the Heart of America's Promise

Will Hoyt

Front Porch Republic *Books*

FEAR AND TREMBLING IN LAS VEGAS
An Unintended Journey to the Heart of America's Promise

Front Porch Republic Books
An Imprint of Wipf and Stock Publishers
199 W. 8th Ave., Suite 3
Eugene, OR 97401

www.wipfandstock.com

PAPERBACK ISBN: 979-8-3852-6971-6
HARDCOVER ISBN: 979-8-3852-6972-3
EBOOK ISBN: 979-8-3852-6973-0

VERSION NUMBER 03/24/26

"John Muir's Journey to the High Sierra" appeared originally as the 1994 Bertha May Bell Andrews Lecture at Bates College, and then, eight months later, as an essay in the Fall 1994 issue of *Caelum et Terra*. "Romano Guardini on Technology," "City Lights, Receding," "Weather Advisory," "America's Deposit of Faith," "Shaken Not Stirred," and "Why Cormac McCarthy Stands Alone Among Novelists" appeared, respectively, in May 1995, Oct 1996, Nov 2021, Jan/Feb 2024, Oct 2024, and July/Aug issues of *New Oxford Review*. "The Humane Vision of Elmore Leonard," "Burning River," and "Ishmael's Real Name was Jonah" appeared in July 2018, September 2017, and August 2020 editions of *University Bookman*. "Regarding Civility" appeared in the Fall 2024 issue of *Local Culture*, and "What You Need to Know About Thoreau," "The Man From Bonwit Teller," and "What Tocqueville Couldn't See" appeared in August 2013, April 2014, and May 2023 editions of *Front Porch Republic*. The author is grateful to these institutions and publications for permission to reprint that material here, in slightly altered form.

"Away back in the Middle Ages people used to go on pilgrimages to the Holy Land, and when people in the villages through which they passed asked where they were going, they would reply, 'A la sainte terre,' 'To the Holy Land.' And so they became known as sainte-terre-ers or saunterers."

—John Muir's gloss on a lecture by Thoreau

"What are these dark days I see in this world so badly bent / . . . killing frost is on the ground and the autumn leaves are gone / I lit the torch and I looked to the east and I crossed the Rubicon."

—Bob Dylan, *Rough and Rowdy Ways*

Contents

Introduction

These essays were written over the course of thirty years starting in 1994 when I was planning a move from California to Ohio. They are the jottings of one who lit out for the territory much as his ancestors did on a floodtide of conviction (widely shared) that America would prove immune to cultural forces eroding Europe's ability to function as a repository of Western civilization, and who arrived at the apex of his professional powers when that same tide, to his surprise and dismay, went back out with ripping force. As such, these essays constitute (upon being presented in chronological order as they are here) a time-lapse photograph of civilizational collapse as experienced by people grounded in eastern Ohio, Detroit, Cleveland, Michilimackinac, and, roughly, just about anywhere between eastern Ohio hill country, where the Cuyahoga (Crooked River) rises, and northern Michigan's western shore, where L'Arbre Croche (Crooked Tree) stands—an assemblage of places that George Grant called the "Great Lake Region of North America."

Will the forty-seventh president of the United States, a man who happily and without irony refers to Jesus as the Christ, restore Western Civilization or at least forestall its collapse? I think not, given Trump's indebtedness to social media and his sworn commitment to serve as commander-in-chief of an empire secured by the strongest armed force on the planet. But, of course, I could be wrong, and in any case this question's answer is incidental to the subject most often under scrutiny in the essays gathered here and, to that extent, to this book's theme—namely, the rise of the technocratic state and its relationship to the false choices that have so clouded our thinking ever since their appearance in the early thirteen century, when the medieval era ended.

I detailed that latter event at some length in a book I published several years ago called *The Seven Ranges*, and my conclusion there was that every single one of those false choices derived from the removal of an integrative center that could still be glimpsed by virtue of an imitative aspect to their falseness. In other words, many of the false choices bedeviling us were to some extent masquerading as real opposites, and that fact, in turn, enabled astute observers to "see" and, in general, orient themselves by the center that had been removed.

In this book I reach a different conclusion, which is that the option of seeing in this latter way appears to be closed. Rather than functioning as a key that enables comprehension, the imitative aspect of false opposites appears to have vanished altogether, and the reason it has vanished is that the imitative aspect has been successful—i.e., perfected to the point where things now simply refer to, or "sign," themselves and nothing else.

Which, of course, would seem to indicate that we are indeed undergoing something like civilizational collapse. Shall we call the event "a corner turned"? That seems better. For there are good aspects to our current situation, and we need to keep those silver linings in view, not least of which is the growing relevance of the American literary inheritance catalogued throughout this book.

Six months ago I was in London, walking between terminals at Heathrow Airport, and I kept hearing a repetitive series of tones in my head. Three step-wise notes: whole step on the bottom, half step on top. The sequence timed well with my breathing so I started humming the tones as I walked so as to steady my gait and keep myself moving toward connecting flights, sometimes on a conveyor belt where I passed people standing, other times on concrete or tile. Then, a few weeks later, I chanced to hear a recording of plainchant featuring *tonus peregrinus*, the so-called "wandering tone," composed by Perotin, music director at Notre Dame Cathedral during the late twelfth century, and I heard in that recording the same series of notes that had steadied me as I walked between terminals in London. So I started to listen closely to the words that were fitted to the tones: *Viderunt omnes termini terrae / salutare Dei nostri*. They were from the ninety-eighth psalm, which celebrates the epiphanic event shepherds keeping watch over their flocks heard angels singing about two thousand years ago—namely, the institution of end time, also known (in Greek) as *kairos*.

A coincidence? Of course.

But that doesn't mean the coincidence was meaningless. Quite the opposite. For me the coincidence was of crucial importance because, humming *viderunt omnes* as I was in the sealed environment otherwise known as an airport, it enabled me to glimpse the new (you might say "final") interpretive construct that, for the next hundred years or so, will surely enable navigation in ways that older, now obsolete interpretive constructs like "faith v. science" or "strong towns v. big tech" can't—the difference between living "inside" the new, completely manufactured technocracy we are building, and living "outside" it in a world not made by us.

A corner turned.

Some persons will no doubt discover this thanks to a different set of circumstances, but lest they don't, or lest they miss that opportunity altogether, my hope is that readers of this book will gain at least some sense of the enormity of the civilizational change presently underway and the brightness of the territory coming into view on our new horizon.

Acknowledgements

Special thanks to Wes Avram who, at great risk to himself, awarded me the chance to deliver the 1994 Andrews Lecture at Bates College; to Marc Barnes who no less graciously provided me with an opportunity to sharpen my essay on James Bond; to Jeremy Beer for inviting me to write about Thoreau in *Front Porch Republic*'s "What You Need to Know" series; to Jeff Bilbro for marvelously quick, on-point editing skills; to Jacob Imam for inviting me to practice briccolage at the 2021 New Polity conference; and to John and Catherine Kuhner, owners of BookMarx Books, for providing me an opportunity to speak at their store about America's "deposit of faith." Additionally I am grateful to Jason Peters for finding time to teach yokels like me how to speak in good English, to Rusty Reno for patiently serving as a sounding board while I sorted out which essay belonged where, to Gerald Russello for allowing me to find my stride as a sharper during his tenure as editor at *University Bookman*, and to Reuben Slife, my son Lucas, and Bill Kauffman for proofreading early and late drafts of the manuscript for errors and thematic integrity. Former neighbor Dale Vree and his son Pieter, successive editors-in-chief at *New Oxford Review*, have both been wonderful to work with over the years, and—thinking now of one dinner party rather than years—I remain deeply indebted to Ken Wear for alerting me to Ian Fleming's detailed salutes to Steubenville in *Casino Royale* and *Diamonds Are Forever*. Last but not least I need to thank Wipf & Stock managing editor Emily Callihan for helping to ensure that this book was formatted on time, and Dr. Robert Coles for providing crucial encouragement as I decided, thirty-five years ago, to write without institutional support and thereby risk becoming the vagrant saunterer or, I should say, holy-lander ("sainte-terre-er") that I turned out, in fact, to be.

I

John Muir's Journey to the High Sierra

North Berkeley 1994

> By the grace of God I am a Christian, by my deeds a great sinner, and by my calling a homeless wanderer of humblest origin, roaming from place to place. My possessions consist of a knapsack with dry crusts of bread on my back and in my bosom the Holy Bible. That is all![1]

These words, famous now the world over as the opening lines to the anonymously-penned nineteenth-century Slavic work *The Way of a Pilgrim,* could serve just as well as an introduction to the Russian peasant's contemporary, John Muir. Moreover, the introduction would be surprisingly complete.

During the fall of 1867, for example, Muir spent his time walking alone through a war-ravaged and often roadless American South toward Florida, a place Muir called "the land of flowers." He started in Indiana and walked thirty miles a day, living on tea leaves and crusts of bread when he could get them, and at other times simply on oats dried by hot stones. His possessions? Comb, towel, soap, plant press, and a copy of *Paradise Lost.* That is all! We know this courtesy of a thief who unpacked Muir's pack somewhere on the west slope of the Alleghenies. He did also carry a Bible, but he didn't really need that; thanks to a feat of memorization performed as a boy, he had much of the New Testament memorized line for line, Matthew to Revelation, in his head. Bands of Confederate guerillas mistook Muir for an herb doctor; others couldn't place him at all.

1. Bacovsin, *Way of a Pilgrim*, 13.

Once, upon asking for lodging at one of the few Cumberland Mountain cabins whose owners had not been driven away or killed during the war, Muir warned the woman of the house and her blacksmith husband that he had only "a five dollar greenback," and that if it was hard for them to make change he would rather go hungry. The blacksmith—"hammer in hand, bare-breasted, sweaty, begrimed, and covered with shaggy black hair"—hesitated, then turned on his heel, and told his wife the stranger was welcome to eat their bread. Later, after saying grace, the blacksmith turned to Muir, asked what he was doing in Tennessee, and learned that Muir was looking at plants. The blacksmith disapproved. "Surely you are able to do something better than wander over the country and look at weeds and blossoms," he said. "These are hard times, and real work is required of every man that is able. Picking up blossoms doesn't seem to be a man's work at all in any kind of times."[2]

It was a dramatic moment, not least because the blacksmith was unaware of just how strong Muir's hand really was. The man didn't know, for example, that Muir could split one hundred rails of fence in a day, or drive a breaking plow behind five oxen and turn two-foot furrows straight as an arrow without the need of steering. Yet Muir mentioned none of this. Rather than capitalize on prowess at skills a blacksmith would respect, Muir played an even stronger card:

> "You are a believer in the Bible, are you not?" "Oh, yes." "Well, you know Solomon was a strong minded man . . . and yet he considered it was worthwhile to study plants; not only to go and pick them up as I am doing, but to study them; and you know we are told that he wrote a book about plants; not only the great cedars of Lebanon, but little bits of things growing between the cracks of walls. Therefore, you see that Solomon differed very much more from you than from me in this matter. I'll warrant you he had many a long ramble in the mountains of Judea, and had he been a Yankee he would likely have visited every weed in the land. And again, do you not remember that Christ told his disciples to 'consider the lilies how they grow,' and compared their beauty with Solomon in all his glory? Now, whose advice am I to take, yours or Christ's? Christ says, consider the lilies. You say, don't consider them. It isn't worthwhile for a strong-minded man."[3]

2. Muir, *Walk to the Gulf*, 23.

3. Muir, *Walk to the Gulf*, 24.

Needless to say, the good blacksmith was silenced. Like those who hosted the Russian pilgrim on his way, this mountain man, after encountering Muir and the strange authority with which he spoke, walked away changed.

Most of us, when we hear the name John Muir, think "conservationist." And rightly so. After all, if it weren't for Muir there might not be any national parks, Yosemite Valley might be owned by mining companies, and Grand Canyon might be the name of a vacation city perched along the real canyon's walls. Not for nothing are redwood groves, Alaskan glaciers, and Yosemite backcountry named after this man. Muir was, as National Park Service brochures point out, a giant in the world of American environmentalism. World-class explorer, adviser and friend to Teddy Roosevelt, author of the learned *Mountains of California*, leading publicist and lobbyist for unspoiled wilderness, glaciologist, founder of the Sierra Club—the list is long, and the titles are all earned. They are also misleading. Concentrate on this aspect of Muir's life and you stand a good chance of missing the real story, the true sense in which Muir is a giant—in short, those aspects of his life that have proved unsettling enough to cause many a student of Muir to run for the shelter of safe talk about how, if Muir could be said to have had a mission, it was to save wilderness "for future generations," or how, if Muir was like a prophet, it was because he liked to portray himself as a kind of John the Baptist in his eagerness to dunk fellow countrymen in nature's beauty, nothing more, yet another of his delightful eccentricities, on par with his ability to subsist on hoarflakes and his predilection for bounding toward rocks toppled by earthquakes instead of away from them. Muir's life, let it be said once and for all, is not chiefly a tale of adventure or selfless, founding-father-type heroism. It is, rather, a tale of call and response, of blindness and insight, of strange defaults and, in his thirty-first year, sheer Pascalian-caliber revelation.

Certainly it is possible to read *The Story of My Boyhood and Youth*, *A Thousand-Mile Walk to the Gulf*, and *My First Summer in the Sierra* as a three-part adventure story. Indeed, you would have a grand time of it, as did the New York dinner party cognoscenti who used to listen, justly rapt, to the story of Muir and his noble canine friend Stickeen on that now-famous Alaskan glacier as night fell. But the journals deserve better. Read them closely, and gradually it becomes clear that Muir's entries are in fact mere coins for his lodging—clues if you will, like traces of red mud or maps opened to a certain page. Together, the journals comprise a stunning document; they belong on a shelf along side Merton's *Seven Storey Mountain* and Newman's *Apologia*. For Muir actually made it to a far country. While he was there he became lit up like a torch, and it is our profound good fortune to be able to look into his journals, uncover some of the light preserved in its pages, and thereby illumine to at least some small degree our own dark way.

If he had been asked, Muir would probably have dated his wanderings from the time a small steel file pierced his right eye while he was adjusting a wheel-making machine in an Indianapolis factory in 1867. That accident temporarily blinded him: for four weeks the only light Muir knew was the voice of children reading to him. When he regained his sight, he turned his back on technological pursuits and resolved to study only God's handiwork. For our purposes, however, a somewhat earlier date would be better. I am thinking of the time Muir received a literal call to wake up.

Muir was sixteen then, living on a Wisconsin farmstead ruled by a stern Calvinistic father. As a boy in Scotland, in the town of Dunbar on the Firth of Forth, Muir was the victim of many a thrashing for an irrepressible, rule-breaking interest in the wilds of bog and meadow; now, as a young man, books were the cause of trouble. Against the wishes of his father, who wanted him to read only Scripture, Muir had begun to thrill to literature in general—Milton, Burns, Sir Walter Scott—and one night, after stealing more reading time than the five or ten minutes allotted to him, Muir's father said that if his son must read he should do it in the morning. Aha! A crack had appeared in the wall of the cell; light was passing through; there was hope. "That night I went to bed wishing with all my heart and soul that somebody or something might call me out of sleep to avail myself of this wonderful indulgence; and next morning to my joyful surprise I awoke before father called me," he wrote. "A boy sleeps soundly after working all day in the snowy woods, but that frosty morning I sprang out of bed as if called by a trumpet blast, rushed downstairs, scarce feeling my chilblains, enormously eager to see how much time I had won, and when I held up my candle to a little clock that stood on a bracket in the kitchen I found that it was only one o'clock. I had gained five hours, almost half a day! 'Five hours to myself!' I said, 'five huge, solid hours!' I can hardly think of any other event in my life, any discovery I ever made that gave birth to joy so transportingly glorious as the possession of those five frosty hours."[4] It was an embarrassment of riches.

4. Muir, *Boyhood and Youth*, 138.

At first he thought he'd continue reading, but then, upon realizing that his father might object to the time it would take to replace the firewood he'd use to stay warm enough to read, Muir decided instead to go to the cellar and start constructing various mechanical devices he had designed in his head while harvesting corn. Within a week he had made the requisite saws and drills, and soon devices themselves started materializing: cogwheels and cams; then latches, thermometers, and lamplighters; finally a small saw mill and an "early-rising machine" designed to set one on one's feet at any given hour. This latter contraption was more for display than use, however, because Muir continued to listen "for the heavenly one o'clock call" and it "never failed."

Though he harbored enormous powers of resolve, exhibited a streak of fierce independence, and was known, when young, to be a "gude fechter," Muir was home-loving and quite shy. Hence it is remarkable that his spirit was not altogether crushed under the weight of his father's joylessness. The farm Muir's father "homesteaded" was in fact built on the broken backs of sons, and John, being the oldest, carried the greatest weight. When a well needed to be dug through ninety feet of limestone, young John was the one chosen to do it, and do it he did, for three straight months. The experience—and it is emblematic of his entire childhood—nearly killed him. At sixty feet Muir unwittingly struck a vein of odorless carbonic gas, and when he was lowered into the well the next morning he lost consciousness; neighbors, after the fact, were shocked that he had found the presence of mind to hold onto his rope long enough to be pulled out and saved. Muir's one comment on the episode—"constant chipping wears away stone; it also wears away the chipper"—speaks volumes. Yet he survived.

When he was a boy in Scotland a nurse loved to tell him that if he persisted in wayward, nest-hunting ways he would be thrown into hell; Muir, picturing the dark, stone-walled dungeon of Dunbar Castle, always replied that he'd climb out. Well, he was right. He did climb out. Two years after sinking the well shaft, Muir collected his best mechanical inventions, said good-bye to his mother and sisters, asked his father if he could turn to him for help should he ever need a loan ("no"), and walked down to the railroad station. What in the world, the conductor wanted to know, were those contraptions in the bag? "Inventions for keeping time, early rising, and so forth." After bending down and studying a clock the conductor's eyes widened and he walked up to the engine to speak with the engineer. "Charlie," he said. "Don't you ever take a passenger? I wish you would take this man on. He has the strangest machines in the baggage car I ever saw in my life. I believe he could make a locomotive. He wants to see the engine running. Let him on."[5] When the engineer finally relented and Muir climbed aboard—headed for an exhibition at a country fair which proved to be a ticket to the University of Wisconsin—one fairly weeps on account of the homespun, whimsical, wildly improbable aspect of his deliverance.

It would make a good ending, this picture of a young man embarking for a county fair, and I will treat it as such, for Muir's life was soon to be marked by an altogether different sort of leaving.

Attending the university in Madison was roughly equivalent to attending paradise for Muir. He learned Latin and Greek, was introduced to Wordsworth and Thoreau, studied geology, and followed Agassiz's theories about glacial activity as a land-shaping force. Every professor he met encouraged him; they all lived in houses overflowing with books; and whenever the weather turned cold everybody kindled hearth fires big enough to cheer even the most dour soul. Most important of all, Muir was introduced to botany. That a locust should be kin to a pea—Muir saw in this fact, not so immediately apparent, a stunning instance of "essential unity with boundless variety," and from that moment forward a plant press became as important to him as a coat. In sum, Muir thrived in Madison, and people began to expect big things of him. His sisters thought he would become an inventor; his mother figured he would wind up in the ministry; professors assumed he could become a professor. Muir, dutifully prompted by a desire to serve his fellow man, settled on medicine. But then a funny thing happened. Just as he was on the verge of professional advancement, right as time became ripe for a proposal of marriage to a suitable young woman he very much liked, Muir stalled. He defaulted. He dropped out, went on a "geological and botanical excursion" along the Mississippi, and then, upon returning, formally quit the university without taking his degree. Back at home, working now for his brother-in-law, Muir was as confused as anyone by his inability to seize "success." He later wrote that he began to doubt in this period whether he was "full born," and clearly this status was to Muir a source of real pain. Then, sometime during the fall of 1863, he reached a pass in his thinking that was every bit as important as the one he crossed when he came upon the "five frosty hours."

In brief, he saw the glorious possibility of going for broke and crossing over, of turning the world on its head and simply becoming what everyone

5. Muir, *Boyhood and Youth*, 149.

worried he might become—namely, a tramp. Over the course of the winter Muir set his affairs in order much as would a man dying. Then, as the first geese appeared (abandoned to divine providence, heading north), Muir left. Like the man who turns not back to get his coat, like a rustle of wind in the grass, he leaped over a small wall and was gone. He aimed north, then east along the south shore of Lake Superior, and then, via islands strung out like stepping stones between Lake Huron and Georgian Bay, into Canada. After that he was for a long time traceable solely by virtue of flower pressings.

Flowers, flowers, flowers. On the evidence of his journals Muir thought everywhere and always in terms of flowers. He breathed them, studied them, dreamed them. As a boy he chewed their seeds to stay awake during sermons. When he was in the high Sierra he chewed their leaves to fight off giddiness while climbing cliffs. He called them "companions," "plant people preaching," "glad children of light," and when he couldn't see them he found a way to see them anyway. Stars, in Muir's journals, are "sky lilies." Sea-coasts are "white-blooming shores," and clouds are "sky-gardens." Most of the time, of course, Muir saw actual flowers—and in all their pedicled, racemed, involucred, stamened, and pistiled glory. Health, for Muir, really was a mind full of flowers. Thus Florida, by virtue of its name, figured in Muir's mind as a kind of promised land, a place "longed and prayed for and oft visited in dreams," and the difficulties he had getting there (losing his sight, overcoming the temptation to devote himself to designing machines) only increased his expectations.

Yet when he actually arrived, four long years after leaving Wisconsin, he was at a loss. Instead of "a close forest of trees, every one flowering and bent down and entangled to network by luxuriant, bright-blooming vines," he found "a flat, watery, reedy coast, with clumps of mangrove and forests of moss-dressed strange trees appearing low in the distance."[6] Muir concluded his first Florida journal entry by thanking God for "His goodness in granting me admission to this magnificent realm," and, though Muir was always sincere, these words of thanks were especially powerful owing to the bass note sounded just moments earlier: "Not a mark of friendly recognition, not a breath, not a spirit whisper of sympathy. . . . I lay down on my elbow eating bread, gazing, and listening to the profound strangeness."[7]

As it turned out, of course, the land of flowers was still to come. Would Muir have recognized it if he hadn't, first, failed to find it? All we know is that

6. Muir, *Walk to the Gulf*, 87.

7. Muir, *Walk to the Gulf*, 88.

six months later he arrived in California almost by accident after a winter-long bout with malaria, that he walked south from San Francisco to Pacheco Pass, and then, poor as he had ever been, owing to recent sickness and the loss of his Florida-based hope, that he raised up his head and looked east. There, spread out before him like a map, he saw "a grand smooth outspread plain, watered by a river." There were salmon in that river, the river flowed from a veritable wall of mountains, and everywhere—"side by side, petal to petal, touching but not entwined" for as far as the eye could see—there were flowers. "Here, here is Florida!" he said. Though it was to take him a full year of lowland explorations before he found out, Muir was more right than he could possibly have known or perhaps even imagined.

On May 24, 1869, exactly one week and three days after Major Powell committed the lives of himself and nine companions to the Colorado River on its course through the Grand Canyon, John Muir embarked for the high Sierra. He didn't go alone; he went as a shepherd in the employ of one Mr. Delaney, along with another more experienced shepherd, a Chinese cook, a Southern Paiute guide, a St. Bernard canine named Carlo, and two thousand sheep. That's a lot of sheep to keep track of; therefore, Muir had more than a little to do, but, luckily for the rest of us, Muir kept a notebook tied to his belt.

When I remarked, earlier, that the notes Muir took on his first trip to the Sierra constitute as strong a document of spiritual transformation as we have, I didn't mean that the notes detail visions like the ones you find in the Book of Revelation. On the contrary (and this is one of the principal reasons we can trust the notes), their province is the plain and the ordinary—what Muir called "nature's open . . . sunny everyday beauty," be it rain "steeping" in "black meadow mold," or the "curved instep of trees bent from the weight of heavy snows," or the cultural benefits of small-scale, as opposed to large-scale, sheep farming. Muir always had an eye for the obvious, for looking at whatever was right in front of him and seeing it afresh, but in his Sierran notes the talent is pronounced. Clothes, different kinds of light, smells, cultural idiocies, landform—as long as it was real it interested him. The other chief reason for the authenticity of Muir's Sierran vision is that he was always in complete possession of his senses when writing. Yes, in this journal Muir proved himself a mystic. But he didn't get that way by closing his eyes. Rather, those eyes were wide open, along with every other cell in his body. Some years later, while attending a social event in Oakland, Muir was invited to participate in a session of "spirit-rapping" and he more than refused; he absolutely ruined the party. "I've been praying all my life, 'Open mine eyes that I may see,'" he said. "Now you tell me to close my eyes, or sit in the dark while somebody goes under the table . . . why, mon, if I'd make such a fool of myself I'd never be able to look a pine tree in the face again!"[8]

At first all he saw on his Sierran journey were "hoofed locusts," as he called his charges. The damage two thousand sheep inflicted as they tumbled eastward astounded him. Soon, though, other phenomena competed for attention: sugar pines, incense cedar, bluebirds, destructive methods of gold-mining. At one point Muir described a kind of lightning he'd never seen before ("white glowing cloud-shaped masses down among the trees and bushes . . . the spreading hair of the horses' tails and sparks from our blankets show how highly charged the air is"); at another, evidently while waiting for snow to melt in the high pastures, Muir catalogued a garden of lilies.

Then things changed. Driving sheep up onto a divide, the group forded Yosemite Creek—the same creek that eventually plunges three thousand feet to the valley floor—and set up camp in the high country.

For Muir it was like walking onto the roof of the world. Leaving the sheep and his companions behind, he walked until he found a place from which to view the entire snow-capped Sierra crest and then returned toward camp, this time walking along the precipice that defines the north wall of Yosemite Valley:

> After a mile or so of this memorable cliff work I approached Yosemite Creek, admiring its easy, graceful, confident gestures as it comes bravely forward in its narrow channel, singing the last of its mountain songs on its way to its fate—a few rods more over the shining granite, then down half a mile in showy foam to another world, to be lost in the Merced, where climate, vegetation, inhabitants are all different. Emerging from its last forge, it glides in wide, lace-like rapids down a smooth incline into a pool where it seems to rest and compose its gray, agitated waters before taking the grand plunge, then slowly slipping over the lip of the pool basin, it descends another glossy slope with rapidly accelerating speed to the brink of the tremendous cliff, and with sublime, fateful confidence springs out free in the air.[9]

8. Wolfe, *Son of the Wilderness*, 172–173.

9. Muir, *First Summer in the Sierra*, 82–83.

Clearly the creek fascinated Muir. Indeed, it fascinated him so much that he took off his shoes and socks and worked his way down to the very brink just described, alongside "booming" water. It turned out to be a false brink. The real brink was on the far side of a small brow "too steep for mortal feet." Even as he made this judgment, however, Muir's eyes were picking out, on the very edge of the brow, a shelf three inches wide ("just wide enough for a rest for one's heels"), and, as if drawn, he crept down to this ledge too. There he obtained "a perfectly free view down into the heart of the snowy, chanting throng of comet-like streamers." Moreover, on his way down to the three-inch-wide shelf Muir had found the presence of mind to note a plant growing in a crack, identify it ("artemisia"), and fill his mouth with its bitter taste.

It wasn't until he returned to camp that Muir fully appreciated the danger he had been in. But realize it he did—and to about the same extent that he realized he had no idea how long he had stayed on the ledge or how he got back up. For several nights in a row he slept fitfully if at all; one time he even woke up shouting. "This time it is real," he apparently said. "All must die."

From that day forward, Muir's diary entries reflect what ought really to be called a change of authorship. Part of the difference, no doubt, is that he had quite literally changed elevations. Whereas before he had been amongst sugar pines and ferns, now he was standing on tundra next to glaciers under a fiercely bright sun. But the bigger difference is personal: he was no longer on the outside looking in.

Whereas before he had described flowers from without, now he appeared to be in one. "The air widens in beauty—like a flower."

Muir had in some sense entered the rose Dante Alighieri tried to write about.

"No pain here," reads an entry dated July 2. "No sense of dead stone, all spiritualized. . . . No fear of the past, no fear of the future. . . . Gift of good God."[10] In the evening, after writing to his mother and a few friends: "They seem as near as if within voice reach or touch. The deeper the solitude the less the sense of loneliness." July 27, after "a run back to camp" of eight or nine miles: "The rocks, the air, everything speaking." At times, Muir himself is the one doing the speaking, and, like Melville who also tracked the glacial whiteness of very God, Muir speaks at those moments in something like tongues, unleashing uncharacteristic torrents of joyous,

10. Muir, *First Summer in the Sierra*, 91.

clearly deranged, always intelligible speech. While considering the various courses available to raindrops, for instance, Muir doesn't just talk of how, "with blunt plap-plap and low bass drumming," some drops "fall on the broad leaves of veratrum, saxifrage, cypripedium." He also says: "creeping through invisible doors into the round room of cells."[11] Most of the time, however, Muir lets landscapes and events do the talking, as when he observes the appearance of a strangely red cloud around Cathedral Peak, or notes how harmoniously related aspects of the Tuolumne watershed glow "like a human face in a glory of enthusiasm." August 2: "Sketching all day on the North Dome until four or five o'clock in the afternoon, when as I was busily . . . trying to draw every tree and every line and feature of the rocks, I was suddenly, and without warning, possessed with the notion that my friend, Professor J.D. Butler of the State University of Wisconsin, was below me in the valley, and I jumped up full of the idea of meeting him, with almost as much startling excitement as if he had suddenly touched me to make me look up." August 3: "Found Professor Butler as the compass needle finds the pole."[12]

Muir stayed in the high Sierra for three years before returning to what most of us would call civilization, and on the evidence of letters and remembrances by friends Muir's line of communication with "very God," as he liked to say, remained unbroken.

During the winter, the time of "fertile snowstorms," Muir holed up in one or another of several sugar pine shake cabins he made for himself on the valley floor and supported himself as a sawyer and a caretaker. Summers he was back up on the "ice-ploughed" divide, hunting and then measuring what glaciers remained and in general exulting like Noah in the new earth so recently brought to light after a very great flood. Except for the company of a mule he was alone; when he came down to the valley floor it was usually just to replenish his supply of bread, and on those occasions when he did meet people they just flat-out couldn't place him. Even friends had this problem. The aforementioned Professor Butler, upon seeing the rough-clad Muir approach, mistook him for the gardener, as it were. "Professor Butler," Muir said, when his face was only inches away. "Don't you recognize me?" It still took the professor quite a few long moments before he finally understood the identity of his questioner. This kind of thing happened all the time to Muir during those years. It wasn't just

11. Muir, *First Summer in the Sierra*, 89.

12. Muir, *First Summer in the Sierra*, 125–128.

that Muir was a workingman who also published articles with titles like "The Death of a Glacier." Nor was it that, owing to his need to protect himself against light itself in higher altitudes, he often showed up with his face smeared with soot. It was his eyes. After seeing a picture of Muir taken in 1870, his brother wrote that the eyes "did not look natural," and it is true: the picture is still extant; anybody can see the uncanniness.

But the main way to appreciate how wilderness put its mark on Muir is simply to trace his wanderings. In 1872 he wrote in a letter that he felt strong enough "to leap Yosemite walls at a bound" and, in truth, he appears to have done something very close to that (via antelope bounds?) on a shockingly regular basis. Perhaps it was the sheer joy in him. Journal entries show him to have traveled distances in a single day that seasoned mountaineers would raise an eyebrow at, and he had strange reserves of strength. On a solo (ropeless) ascent of the east face of Mt. Ritter in October 1872 Muir got stuck half way up. He was at his weakest—both arms outstretched—and no new foothold was in sight. "Faith and hope failed," he later related. "Cold sweat broke out. My senses filled as with smoke. I was alone, cut off from all affinity. Would I fall to the glacier below? Well, no matter. . . . Then as if my body, finding the ordinary dominion of mind insufficient, pushed it aside, I became possessed of a new sense. My quivering nerves, taken over by my other self, instinct, or guardian angel—call it what you will—became inflexible. My eyes became preternaturally clear, and every rift, flaw, niche, and tablet of the cliff ahead were seen as through a microscope."[13] A short while later he was on the summit.

That in November of this same year Muir did fall, that after coming down "off the mountain" for a two-week stay in San Francisco he returned to discover the Sierra silent and "untalkative," that for the rest of his life stones would "speak" only in proportion to Muir's talents as a writer and a naturalist—all that is but further proof that Muir climbed a holy mountain.

It is said that Muir was a transcendentalist, that if one is to understand John Muir one must first understand the language of transcendentalism. I say: rubbish. No doubt Muir would have been content with the label; if he could be said to be a follower of anyone it would have been Ralph Waldo Emerson, and when he started to write for public consumption he did increasingly substitute words like "Nature" or "Beauty" for "God" or "the Lord," which of course most critics like because this tendency enables us to explain the broad success of Muir's later, conservation-oriented

13. Muir, *The Mountains of California*, 64–65.

thought as the fruit of "maturation." But are we really sure that the Christian "phraseology" of Muir's younger years was just a "holdover" from his father's tutelage? I submit that even where Muir's transcendentalist rhetoric is sharp, Muir was never anything but a slightly reconstructed Christian, if he can be said to have been reconstructed at all. Wherein lies the false note: does it sound when Muir (in his journal) thanks "the Lord" with "all his heart"? Or when Muir (while writing an article) writes that when you look at mountains "you lose consciousness of your own separate existence, blend with the landscape, and become part and parcel of nature?" The truth of the matter is that, his preference for tea over wine notwithstanding, Muir had a whole lot more in common with someone like Belloc than Emerson. Muir's strong suit isn't the Oversoul; it's his intuitive understanding of perennial philosophy.

In the end, though, it is Muir's own life—the shape of it—that speaks loudest. Servanthood, pilgrimage, a walk to a southern clime in a thirty-first year! Logos is written all over him. It's a remarkable thing. With most people, you have to hunt around a little to see spiritual structure. It's there, but you have to read between the lines a little to get at it. In Muir's case you have the opposite problem. Here, the archetypal pattern is so obvious that you actually stand in danger of missing it simply because you don't expect the script to be that large, that plain, that visible. The letters are all capitals. All you need do, in order to read them, is give yourself over to a kind of glorious literalism and everything falls into place. No reading between the lines, no Jungian analysis, just events: climbing out of hell, wake-up calls, blindness then sight. And at journey's end? What else but a mountain called "Cathedral Peak." When Muir (in his journal) actually gets to the "roof" and starts admiring "the masonry" evident in "the gable on the northeast end," a reader is apt to feel that he or she has passed through a looking glass. And there are other equally meaningful moments that I haven't mentioned—events like the baptism that occurred when Muir almost drowned in a pond. However, for sheer signifying power none of these moments quite matches what occurred on Muir's walk through Georgia when, after being "filled with indescribable loneliness," he bathed "in a black, silent stream," approached a graveyard outside of Savannah on a "smooth white shell road," and drank from a "dull, sluggish, coffee-colored stream" before finding a little mound that served for a pillow, going to sleep, and then discovering, upon waking, that he had been lying on a grave.[14]

14. Muir, *Walk to the Gulf*, 75.

A short while ago I said Muir reminded me of Belloc. In point of fact, the personage with whom Muir shares most is St. Francis, who, like Muir, was also consigned by his father to a lightless pit. And who else addresses flowers and bears and planetary bodies as if they were peers? "Plant people," "fellow mortals"—phrases like these accord with the vision immortalized in Francis' *Canticle of the Sun*.

Note too that even their physiques were similar: not tall, slight in build, enormous vivacity and quickness. Mostly, though, I think of their poverty—that "uncompromising destitution" (borrowing from Merton here) "which alone can give joy because it flings one headlong into the arms of God." Like Francis, Muir inherited five frosty hours and counted himself rich! Muir, in other words, was the penultimate poor man, the man who ran on empty, burned his bridges, and spent everything he had. Some, when hearing his name, see him standing next to President Roosevelt across the valley from Yosemite Falls; others see him in Alaska on a glacier with the noble mongrel Stickeen. I for my part tend to see him on those first few days after he left Wisconsin as a twenty-five year-old, loping east past the Apostle Islands along the south shore of Lake Superior. Alone, with only a compass to guide him; a few crusts of bread in his pack; plant press strapped on top. John Muir was poor then and therefore free—as abandoned to divine providence as the very geese overhead.

II

Romano Guardini on Technology

East Bay Hills 1995

At the turn of the previous century, Hilaire Belloc walked through a Europe that no longer exists and wrote a book about his journey. Called *The Path to Rome*, the book stands for many of us as one of the few great windows onto a pre-technocratic, Christ-drenched culture that was truly, even gloriously, at home on earth. Canals with working tow paths, early morning woodsmoke, mountain huts, bread, oxcarts, wine. Perhaps because Belloc wrote so quickly (he wrote as fast as he walked and with the same reckless abandon), the book has an unstudied character that serves it well in its unintended role as a memorial. Yet the reader will look in vain should he turn to Belloc for a glimpse of Lake Como in northern Italy, beneath the Alps. Yes, Belloc passed through Como. Yes, he provides luminous details about life to the north and south. But of Lake Como itself he says nothing, and for the simple reason that it was too beautiful, too right, too integrated into the land that sustained it. Belloc calls the place "music," says a quick prayer lest the region bewitch him, and then marches on toward Rome. I bring this up because Romano Guardini, writing twenty-three years later in letters mailed from Lake Como, also calls the place "music."

To the Italian-born but German-raised Guardini the Lake Como region was "a landscape in which all the risings and fallings and measures and proportions came together in one clear melody," and, like Belloc, he found the sight of it overpowering: "Everywhere it was inhabited land.... All nature had been given a new shape by us humans. What culture means in its narrowest sense struck me with full force. The lines of the roofs merged from different directions. They went through the small town set on the hillside or followed the windings of the valley. Integrated in many ways, they finally reached a climax in the belfry with its deep-toned bell. All these things were caught up and encircled by the well-constructed mountain masses."[1]

Rather than simply crossing himself and moving on, however, this visitor stayed for a while before walking on toward Rome. Factories had appeared since Belloc was there, and Guardini, horrified, felt compelled to track down the implications. Hence these letters. "Here was nature indwelt by humanity," he explains to a friend. "And now I saw it breaking apart. . . . The world of natural humanity, of nature in which humanity dwells, was perishing. I cannot tell you how sad this made me."[2]

We have heard a lot in recent years about the end of nature—by which people mean the great outdoors insofar as it has been untouched by man—and there has been a lot of public grieving on this score, as if to say that the passing of this concept was something of moment. Certainly ecological devastation is of moment. But the idealization of untouched nature is merely a romanticism—the flipside, so to speak, of more frankly exploitative energies, for both phenomena are premised on the erroneous idea that humans are separate from nature and in some sense above it. In truth, there never has been any such thing as untouched nature; nature was changed the moment humans appeared on earth, and we for our part have always been, well, natural. The real issue, then, as even The Nature Conservancy now understands, is the loss of sustainable place-ripened *cultures* in which human and non-human nature both flourish. This, at any rate, is the loss Guardini is trying to gauge in his letters from Lake Como. Guardini's name for the culture under siege is "Urbanitas," which he defines as a mode of being in which "a rhythm soars over everything" and man's creations blend harmoniously with the landscape into which they're set. Another name for it might be "agriculture"—culture that is as much land-shaped as it is land-shaping. But whatever you call it, any and all analyses of what has happened are of importance.

Guardini's analysis, it turns out, is of particular importance—first because he was situated right at the turning point and able to look both ways, second because he saw and wrote so well. It is true that his conclusions are off. Indeed, they are very off. But they are still (by virtue of their

1. Guardini, *Letters from Lake Como*, 5.

2. Guardini, *Letters from Lake Como*, 6.

failure) instructive, and, thankfully, they have now been grouped together and published in book form as an entry in the Ressourcement Series. The book's subtitle is *Explorations in Technology and the Human Race*.

The book is arranged very simply: nine letters, circa 1923–1925, and then a transcript of a talk delivered in 1959. The letters appear in their original form and order, and there is no commentary. They don't need it, as the letters are held together by a strong sequential thread. I say "sequential." In fact, the meaning in this book tends to grow according to cumulative rather than serial logic. The overall effect is one of circling and re-circling. Guardini watches and waits and slowly builds up understanding by starting in each letter from the same point—namely, the appearance of a box-like factory amidst "the singing lines of a small town." The last letter is a little different; there he zooms off in a straight line and never looks back. But until that point Guardini proceeds by circling.

He begins, during his first two revolutions, by noting the differences between artifacts like steamships and sailboats. Next, under headings like "consciousness," "abstraction," and "the masses," Guardini tries to get a read on the order that is coming—an order that he prefers to think of as simultaneously un-cultural and unnatural. Guardini's consideration of "abstraction," in which he talks about the various degrees of withdrawal required to design and operate technology, seems a little thin to me, but his meditation on mass culture, despite a decidedly patrician bias, is strong. Like Kierkegaard, Guardini shows how, in the world to come, people will become individuals ("persons") solely to the extent that they leap over the blade of a leveler directly into the arms of God. There is also a strong section on the difference between the kind of knowing that has been abroad in the world since Bacon (manipulative, extractive, coercive) and the kind of knowing whose aim is to "penetrate, move within, live with." By noting how both kinds of knowing are modes of desire, Guardini reminds us that the theory with the greatest explanatory power, when it comes to diagnosing ills deriving from the rise of technocracy, is the Book of Genesis.

But the best sections in *Letters from Lake Como* are the grounded ones, the sections where Guardini turns away from speculative talk and tries instead to register topography—the culture-scape, if you will—that was right before his eyes. Here I think particularly of his eighth letter, where he tries for the last time to take the measure of stone walls, vineyards, arbors, and rooftops so perfectly integrated into the land they define that, as a beholder, one's only choice is to erase the imaginary line that divides land-based cultures from entities like deserts and oceans and call the whole business Creation. "Every so often there are stairways, shallow steps with round stones, making it possible for donkeys with their burdens to climb the hill. How these paths climb and turn. . . ."[3] You'd expect, given the circumstances, that Guardini's words here would be driven by pity, or nostalgia, or even just honest memorialization. But they aren't. They are driven by wonder.

Then along comes the ninth letter and the book falls apart. "There is a yes to what is happening historically," he says. And: "We must not oppose what is new and try to preserve a beautiful world that is perishing." Fair enough, the reader is apt to say, even if he or she does get a little wary here. Certainly we can't live in the past. A few lines later, though, there is this: "We must not oppose what is happening. . . . Nor is it true that what is taking place is not Christian. . . . Only those who had been influenced by the immediacy of the redeemed soul to God . . . could have broken free from the tie to nature."[4] Uh oh. At this point I begin to ride Guardini's prose like an unwilling surfer on a large wave. I sense the facile (therefore dangerous) punchline coming; I know it is going to break with full force, yet I have no choice but to ride it out. Modern technology, Guardini finally claims, is destructive not because it serves and abets our presumption to godlike status but because it is *raw material that has not yet been tamed*. "We have to become lords of the unleashed forces,"[5] he proclaims, thereby surrendering to the very romanticism (and ecological philistinism) he earlier avoided. In letters one through eight Guardini speaks like a resistance fighter. Now, in the ninth, he invites everyone to follow "the inwardly foreshadowed path to the very end, the path of knowledge and growing awareness, of surveying and mastering and technologically transforming nature as it is immediately given."[6]

What, a reader may justly ask, has happened?

What has happened is that prior to writing this last letter Guardini returned to Germany. Despite a clear distaste for Wagner, Guardini was now stirred by thoughts of a coming Third Reich (millenarianism, take two) founded on a "Germanic essence"[7] that can bring to completion

3. Guardini, *Letters from Lake Como*, 70.
4. Guardini, *Letters from Lake Como*, 80–81.
5. Guardini, *Letters from Lake Como*, 82.
6. Guardini, *Letters From Lake Como*, 83–85.
7. Guardini, *Letters from Lake Como*, 86.

Christendom itself. Consider the German youth movement, he suggests. Though German youths "no longer stand eye to eye with nature," they now (in 1929) show another, "equally powerful" form. "Our blood," he explains, "responds to its force,"[8] and in that very instant he substitutes the volkish ideology of "blood and soil" for the agrarian rootedness that the previous eight letters implicitly advocated for.

Needless to say, one wishes there was another, following letter, and it makes sense that editors at the American office of *Communio* would want to position Guardini's 1959 talk, "The Machine and Humanity," as a kind of makeshift tenth letter. But that speech is dull, and, even worse, it suggests that Guardini's views weren't appreciably changed during the intervening years, that he wasn't rocked by the Holocaust any more than Heidegger was. Maybe less! Heidegger at least renounced "mastery" in favor of watching, waiting, and an intellection of ear. Never mind that his kind of watching and waiting may have had more than a little to do with the watching and waiting that an arsonist knows when he or she settles in to see what happens next. My point is that Heidegger's post-1945 writing at least shows an awareness that the Holocaust was an event of enormous significance. That Guardini's writing, on the evidence of his 1959 address, does not reflect this kind of awareness causes the reader to doubt the mind that produced the Lake Como letters and, by extension, the integrity of the letters themselves. Which is too bad, since Guardini clearly was shaken by the Holocaust. The letters deserve better.

I suggest that readers skip "The Machine and Humanity" and go instead to the third chapter of *The End of the Modern World*, a book Guardini penned three years earlier in 1956, for this text is as lively as the 1959 talk is dead and seems to be the piece that the letters from Lake Como pointed toward:

> The last decades have suggested what life without Christ really is. . . . As far as being is nature or the non-personal creation, being belongs to God, whose will is expressed in the laws by which this being, this nature, exists. As far as being is taken out of nature and into the sphere of human freedom, it belongs to man and man is responsible for it. If man fails in his responsibility and does not care for being as he should, it . . . becomes the possession of something anonymous.[9]

8. Guardini, *Letters From Lake Como*, 91.

9. Guardini, *The End of the Modern World*, 83.

With that trenchant summary Guardini is off and moving, and he misses nothing. He acknowledges the Holocaust for the central event it is, points to the growing ecological crisis, anticipates the appearance of biotechnology, and predicts that the loss of reverence "toward the person *qua* person" will be the principal mark of the world to come. Moreover, he suggests how these phenomena and the death of Lake Como are related. All told, it's a slam-dunk hole-in-one home-run type of chapter, sobering yet empowering in the best sense, and therefore the perfect coda to *Letters from Lake Como*.

For there are no good things to be said about the destruction of Lake Como. You can't argue that the first eight letters are a warning sign, or a triangulation point by which to orient ourselves as we shore up failing foundations, or even a map for reconstuction. How do you rebuild something that grew over the course of one thousand years? Only God builds on that scale. The disappearance of Lake Como is a loss, pure and simple. If Guardini's book has value—and it has enormous value—it's because it helps us see the scale of our present-day impoverishment.

City Lights, Receding

Steubenville 1996

Step back in time, just for a moment, and try to think of the universe as a poem. Not in the sense of something lofty or uplifting but in the sense of something that grounds us.

Granted, this maneuver is a bit of a stretch, but given that it was a common grade-school exercise at the school I attended as recently as twenty-five years ago, I am pretty sure it can still be done. Very well, then: the universe as a lettered artifact spoken the way Homer or a Navajo singer might speak. What does it mean to think in this way? Never mind, for the time being, all the ways in which words help us to recognize and then celebrate the luminous aspect to singulars. The main thing to be noticed about the world, when it gets conceived as a poem, is that it can't be said in any other way. Its "sense" is incarnated in the "sound," the string of vocables that conveys the sense. You can't sum up a poem. You can't extract some kernel, call it "content," and from there on out think of the language in which it's couched as decoration.

Now fast-forward over the past quarter-century to the present and think of the world as an information array—the kind you hope to see (hardware permitting) when you turn on your computer and the display terminal lights up. Has anything changed? At first glance, no. After all, the experience of watching the ocean at Big Sur doesn't appear to be changed in the least upon learning that the ocean is an information array. Indeed, you could even argue that when you see that ocean on a computer screen it seems to have an intense "thereness" that is missing when one stands alone and tired on a beach. Yet, that ocean is not there, on a computer screen, the way the ocean is there when you say "ocean." For what you're seeing on your computer is programmed. The gulls you see, the kelp and booming surf—all that is an infinitely reproducible, therefore thoroughly expendable, sequence of binary switches.

Though Norbert Wiener's breakthrough book, *Cybernetics: Control and Communication in the Animal and the Machine,* was published just a couple years before 1950, his thoughts regarding the ways in which positive feedback loops enable adjustment and, therefore, steerage ("cybernetics," as a word, is descended from a Greek term used by Plato that means "good at steering") have permanently changed the way we think. Over a span of just the next forty years the study of teleological "mechanisms" has become the reigning science of our time, and the world it is making possible is already in view. Instead of aiming toward death through a world of yew trees and consonants and factories that belch acrid smoke, we increasingly inhabit a digitalized world in which embodiment simply does not figure at all. Some call this brave new world "neo-biological"; others call it "post-biological."

You would think that ecologists and backpacking enthusiasts would never tolerate the replacement of nature by computerized images. You would think that those of us who lobby on behalf of "earth" and publicize ills deriving from nuclear power plants and eight-row corn threshers would also question the worth of satellite-assisted computer networks. But we don't. Why? It's not so much that we mistake computers for "clean" technology, true though this may be. (No smokestacks. Modems alleviate traffic jams. Toxic waste resulting from silicon chip production is by and large hidden from view.) It's that allegedly earth-loving people subscribe now to the very same informational logic that the most exploitative biotech firm depends on. The very word "ecosystem" is a product (circa 1950) of the computational sciences. The word functions for most of us as a keystone, should we want to summon up a vision of wholeness and health, yet it derives from mathematical modeling projects designed to forecast economic yields. And this is no freak convergence, either. Green disciplines like biological field theory depend heavily on computer-driven means to mathematize whatever gestalt is at hand. No less revealingly, the word "Gaia"—already a flagship term for so-called deep ecologists around the globe—was resurrected from the halls of Greek mythology by a NASA scientist who was struck by how the biosphere behaved according to cybernetic principles. And then there is the other side of the picture, the story of how computer scientists and bioengineers have begun to think organically and holistically. The architects in cellular communications, software design, even robotics—these folks don't exactly think in Newtonian terms. Rather, they think in terms of tree shapes (binary logic is tree logic), hedgerows (unplanned life forms occur along fringes), and beehives (hives are models of distributed consciousness).

Ought it to surprise us, then, that incarnational life is receding?

Thanks to fiber optics and digitalized sensory immersion systems, a new (prosthetic) celestial city is under construction, and not a few of us already live on-site year-round.

Twelve years ago William Gibson wrote a sci-fi novel called *Neuromancer*, in which he tries to visualize a web of connectivity stretching from Atlanta to New York that had only recently come into view. He names that zone "cyberspace" and describes it as follows:

> A consensual hallucination experienced daily by billions of legitimate operators, in every nation. . . . A graphic representation of data abstracted from the banks of every computer in the human system. Unthinkable complexity. Lines of light arranged in the non-space of the mind, clusters and constellations of data. Like city lights, receding.[1]

It's an often-quoted passage, and for good reason: just about everybody has begun to realize that, far from being some futuristic mindscape inhabited by hackers trained in video arcades, the city Gibson saw is increasingly a place that most of us feel comfortable calling home.

Consider: once wired, once plugged into the phone-TV-computer machine, we all communicate with each other instantly, at the speed of light, no matter how far apart our stations may be. Communication isn't so much a matter of speed in this context as it is a matter of simultaneity. As the guys on the floor of the New York Stock Exchange put it, the whole net happens at once. Moreover, owing to the advent of stereoscopic and interactive data-based worlds so complete that one literally enters them, our bodies are now disposable. It's as though they have become suits of clothes, really, just temporary physical co-ordinates (marketable, of course) that you dress up in. Look at us! We have become pure intelligence—omniscient, weightless, smart-like-missiles-are-smart and to that very extent given over to an endless dance of feedback and adjustment, an ecstasy of ever-tightening cybernetic

1. Gibson, *Neuromancer*, 51.

loops. People talk about life-extension fads such as cryonics and interventive gerontology and efforts to download consciousness as if they were the work of a way-out lunatic fringe, and—who knows—maybe they are, for surely it's a little crazy to be working toward a goal that has already been reached. Isn't the drive toward immortal life the drive toward disembodied life, that is to say, the transcendence of corporeal nature and its attendant states of vulnerability, decay, limitation, and change? To the extent that it is, immortality can now be said to be an option. Go "on line" and right away you are on the other side of space and time, *sub specie aeternitis*.

It can be a pleasing life, living like an angel. True, you lose some individuality when you take on anyone-anywhere status, but that is offset by real advantages such as vastly increased power, freedom from material cares, and (on the somewhat ignoble side) access to "evidence." Indeed, life is so good in cyberspace that most of us never even notice it's a trap.

There is an exit, of course. And the door is wide open. Its name? Death. Or, rather, the acceptance of death. It seems odd to talk of death as a door to health, yet it's even odder not to. For you don't have to dig very deep into our Western heritage to see that once upon a time nearly every village in all of Christendom was built around a master sign that actually advocated death. That sign was a crucifix, and what it meant was this: "So, you want to be gods? Very well. Here on this cross is God. Be like Him. Accept ordainment to incarnated status and die. That is the way toward life." It's a pretty clear road sign, that, and close enough (sequentially) to our own, post-Christian time that the peculiar relevance of the idea it presents ought to be clear. Yet it is unclear—so much so that contemporary culture critics ignore the sign entirely.

Can blindness like this just derive from discomfort with religious themes? To me it seems no less likely that it is due to the power of the gravitational force exerted by the new celestial city we're now drawn to.

Almost all films made by Wim Wenders are good, but there is one that I like very much called *Wings of Desire*. It's about an angel who wants to become human. The conceit is very Rilkean. During the first part of the film you watch this denizen of an invisible world hover above a crowd of people hard at work in, well, a library. The angel has at his command all the powers you would expect: freedom from spatial and temporal constraints, the ability to know people's thoughts, unending life. Yet he also hungers for earthly life. He wants to know what it's like to take a bath, experience the peace of a loved one asleep in the next room, wind up with blackened fingers after reading a newspaper. Though already a creature of light, he has begun to suspect that the source of light is the strange condition of embodiment, and soon he finds himself possessed by a desire to cross over and walk the earth as a man. There is just one hitch: no going back. If he crosses over he will die. Should he go? He is unsure, but then a window of opportunity opens, and before he even thinks to go back for a hat he passes through and commences life as a human. He embarks, in other words, on what Flannery O'Connor would have called an education toward death.

Well, that movie is about us. Should we relinquish ersatz angelic status, trust like trees in God-breath, and go "plain"? Or continue to upgrade our anti-death systems and stay "wired"?

It's as though we're at a river. On the one side, the side we're presently on, there is neo-biological civilization, re-presentation via TV, and a form of life that never comes to a close. On the other side there is re-presentation via words, and life that ripens toward the end that is death. Like the difference between pity and compassion, these two sides have the same look but are in fact as different from each other as night and day. The information-based side we're on is a kind of shadowgraph that points by virtue of its very presence to the existence of another, more mortally oriented side. If ever you really see the lay of the land, you can't help but pose the question the Rilkean angel posed: do I cross over? Or stay?

Most of us, I'm sure, would choose to stay where we are. And for good reasons. But a few people, I feel sure, would decide to cross over. What, you can't help wonder, would they find? There are probably as many answers to this question as there are people, but I venture to hope that for at least some the moment of arrival on the other side would be a lot like what Wim Wenders imagined.

I like to think that if ever a group of people should cross over they will find themselves talking to a man named Peter. (In the movie, the first person the former angel befriends is the actor Peter Falk.) The air will be stinging cold, but there will be a stand nearby that sells coffee. "This is good," the newly arrived immigrants will say after Peter offers each of them a cup, and they will stamp their feet and then blow down onto the hot coffee in order to bring the steam up. At this Peter will smile. "Yeah," he will agree, "it's good." And when he says that, when he acknowledges the immigrants' hunger and the goodness of the hot black drink cradled in their cold hands, I think the newcomers' faces will shine. "We could use coats," they will say. Or: "How hard the ground is!" Will they be complaining? I think they will be saying stuff like this for the sheer joy of it. That is why their faces shine! Like two-year-olds breaking through for the first time into the world of speech, these pilgrims will have caught on to the fact that things have names, that upon saying names you behold things in common with the person you are speaking to and then can see them for the corporeal all-there sources of light that they are. Reality itself, in other words, will have bloomed. The entire world will have become a garden of signs.

What You Need to Know About Henry David Thoreau

Harbor Springs 2013

Thoreau can try your patience.

He has a fine mind, and when he trains the light of that mind on a person who thinks at a different, usually slower, speed he is too often inclined to laugh at that person's expense. Upon being invited by an Abenaki guide to speculate on how a hunter could have killed a cow-moose as big as Mt. Kineo, which looms over Moosehead Lake, Thoreau winks at his reader ("whereupon a man-of-war to fire broadsides into her was suggested, etc.") and then mercilessly joins mirth to summary judgment of the guide's attempt to retell the Abenaki myth explaining Mt. Kineo's shape: "An Indian tells such a story as if he thought it deserved to have a good deal said about it, only he has not got it to say, and so he makes up the deficiency by a drawling tone, long-windedness, and a dumb wonder which he hopes will be contagious."[1]

The racist aspects of that remark are not entirely atypical, for in addition to Native Americans Thoreau was inclined to see Irish immigrants and Catholics in general as servants. But the main way in which Thoreau irritates is his unthinking dismissal of "commerce" as a platform for the cultivation of genuinely human life, his customary blindness to the idea that "wildness," so called, might include agriculture as well as life-forms on unvisited mountain peaks, and his uncritical acceptance of the tremendously

1. Thoreau, *Walden and Other Writings*, 513.

destructive nature v. civilization dynamic that had recently energized the growth of the trans-Allegheny West.

And I haven't even gotten to his fondness for yoga, Basmati rice, and elfin spirits that "recline on sunbeams."

Suffice it to say that many if not most contemporary readers of Thoreau reach a point where they are inclined to throw his entire corpus out the window.

What stops them?

Usually it is fear of rashness, for most people never actually read ubiquitously anthologized works like *Walden* and "Civil Disobedience."

Here, though, an opportunity arises. In the wink of an eye belonging neither to themselves nor to Thoreau, readers can become intrigued by what Thoreau might have said to earn a place on the Modern Library roster of giants. Having made a decision to chuck Thoreau entirely they are suddenly free to pick up *Walden* or "Civil Disobedience" as though the manuscripts were messages in a bottle. And after that tipping point is reached, hair usually starts to stand on end, for it quickly becomes clear that Thoreau's pedantry and Yankee practicality and best instincts are each of them in the service of a most wondrous end, which is to report how heaven works, via a detailing of its cogs and gears and nuts and bolts.

The wild, in Thoreau's writings, doesn't just refer to "forest uninterrupted" or country "not yet settled." Ultimately it refers to a place of moral summons and abundant meaning and verbal underpinning that is referred to, variously, as "upriver," "brine," "the eye of the world," even (to the extent incarceration is unjust) "jail." And when he speaks from that wild place—as he does most triumphantly in *Walden* and "Civil Disobedience"—Thoreau winds up redeeming our entire American project, let alone the seemingly more modest ones he undertook in the Maine woods, on the beaches of Cape Cod, and outside Concord, close to Walden Pond.

Take *The Allegash and East Branch* (of the Penobscot), Thoreau's most mature "travel" book, wherein we are invited to glide down a glassy river that presents as "a regularly inclined plane." (Thoreau worked, off and on, as a surveyor.) Here almost every single one of Thoreau's uncritically assumed dichotomies is eventually transposed and enabled to sound in unanticipated senses. Instead of disdain for "civilization," we find localized cultural artifacts like word clusters noted as dutifully as resinous pitch pockets and white-throated sparrows, and instead of disdain for how "the street" sullies Nature's temple, we find sympathetic studies of timber merchants waiting for a "freshet," and hustlers who cut hay on every possible rush-grass island meadow so that they can make a killing from loggers whose oxen will need fuel, come winter.

It's a wise, dare I say "settled," book, yet the source of that bracingly settled aspect is the set of field notes called "Kataadn" (written during Thoreau's stay at Walden Pond), as well as "Civil Disobedience" (written two years after). In "Kataadn," a friend cries out that "the world is on fire" upon witnessing a fir tree ignite, and Thoreau himself likens the summit of Maine's highest mountain to "raw materials of a planet dropped from an unseen quarry," before becoming frightened (indeed, scared out of his wits) by the stunning reality of extant things—of *being*: "Daily to be shown matter, to come into contact with it—rocks, trees, wind. The solid earth! The actual world! Contact! Contact!"[2]

As for "Civil Disobedience," that is the book where Thoreau explains (with ripping, unanswerable clarity) how to disable a "tyranny of the majority" and thus *preserve* a Union in which—as Thoreau himself conclusively demonstrated on July 4, 1845 (the date he began his Walden project)—every man has access to the same kind of contemplative leisure that Plato and Aristotle knew.

Needless to say, there is more going on here than de-activating a Facebook account or starting a program called Simple Living.

Thoreau is our one, absolutely indispensable American man of letters. He faces east! I don't mean he looks toward India. I mean he's a watchman for morning—which is to say, for the human person and things blazing with there-ness. Given that we Americans now live in a counterfeit world of Anthropologie-anchored "villages," genetically-engineered "nature," and ersatz bit-driven "literacy," the good news that Thoreau sends is most welcome.

It amounts to just six words (spoken after finally sounding the pond on whose rim his hojoki-like hut was built): "There is a solid bottom, everywhere."[3]

2. Thoreau, "Kataadn," 80.

3. Thoreau, *Walden and Other Writings*, 256–259.

The Man From Bonwit Teller

Pittsburgh 2014

As Mary Eberstadt has pointed out, evidence is accumulating that the current day usage of pornography is taking a toll on marriages and families. And, as Reinhard Hütter has added, it is also becoming clear that regular pornography consumption results from, and underwrites, a form of spiritual torpor and listlessness that ancient thinkers called *acedia*. Hence it is now possible for critics of porn to say "I told you so" with the same degree of conviction that porn advocates redouble efforts to explore yet another frontier in the mechanics of eroticization. End of story? Perhaps it should be, given that most other discussions about porn result in a push-and-shove battle between people who believe the appearance of porn is a sign of cultural depravity, and others who believe the phenomenon has been evident in strong societies as well as weak ones since the beginning of time.

I wonder, though, if there isn't another, possibly more productive way of thinking about the meaning of porn that is usually unavailable or at least hidden from view, given porn's more obviously sensational aspect. For porn isn't, ultimately, about sex. Rather, porn has to do with immediacy. It comes to pass, it gets enacted if you will, whenever and wherever people provide access to the literally unspeakable and in that way lose their only sure access to a zone most of us naïvely or perhaps not so naïvely refer to as "the real."

Where does it come from, this pull toward immediacy? What are its historical causes?

Richard Weaver famously traced interest in immediacy to the appearance of nominalism in the early fourteenth century, when William of

Occam first devalued the conceptual aspect to words, but for our purposes, here, it would probably make more sense to simply remind ourselves of our identity as Americans—which is to say, our tendency to think that "truth" and "the thing itself" reside on the other side of a constructed metaphor, essay, speech act, or story. As Tocqueville documented, we Americans read newspapers in order to get information, and if we can do that quicker or more efficiently without words, so much the better. Hence we are predisposed to go "visual," and once daguerreotypes appeared we upped the ante still further by turning principally to photographs to get our information, rather than to paintings with their brush strokes, or sketches with their wobbly lines. With a photograph you get almost perfect transparency, and the fictitious thing-in-itself is brought tantalizingly near! Much as a balsam matrix, cover-glass, or microscope invites a viewer to almost feast on the clarity of a biological specimen, so too do photographs create an illusion of almost ecstatic "actuality." Hence we began to return, time and time again, to the photograph, and that habit, in turn, makes for a "new" one, which is the desire to feast on whatever is explicit, edgy, or raw. Sometimes the subject luring our attention is sex. Sometimes it is suffering or humiliation. At other times it is birth, and one day, perhaps, it will be death. But whatever form that rawness takes, we Americans have historically aspired to taste it, and starting in 1962 in New York City we began also to know it and even systematically revel in it as the sheer blast of frightful immediacy that it is.

Most of us are familiar with Greenwich Village neo-folk, the offshoot of Alan Lomax's interest in musical "roots," and John Hammond's promotion of Bob Dylan's first album. What is less often known is that this interest in roots was directly related to the appearance, in gay circles, of a fondness for "kitsch"—which is to say, artistic efforts (velvet paintings, early ads, socialist propaganda) whose sentimentality, tackiness, and obvious falseness put them in a class of their own and even compelled attention as a kind of hotbed for the cultivation of irony. Raw (unmediated) folk "expression" on the one hand, patently decorative (clearly non-revelatory) art on the other—these fads fueled one another thanks to a kind of oscillatory dynamic, and, as such, their simultaneous appearance indicated the removal of art that effectively transmuted, or "heightened," the materials of ordinary experience. I do not mean to say that certain artists working within these two movements did not, in the end, transcend their medium. (Here I think of Dylan's marvelous "free-wheeling" songs, let alone the Chess Records sound he later drew from, and too of Susan

Sontag's marvelous camp-influenced essays.) Rather, I am talking about the movements proper, the collective leanings they represent, leanings that were soon to be dramatically evident thanks to an exhibition of paintings staged (in November, 1962) at the Sidney Janis Gallery on East 57th St, a short taxi ride north and east of Greenwich Village.

That show featured works by a range of mostly American artists who were reacting against abstract impressionism and instituting, in its stead, a new kind of frankly representational painting that depended on found "objects" like mass-produced images. Given that Jackson Pollock et al. were the ruling class in the art world at the time, this Janis show would have made a splash in any case, but in November 1962 the baton-passing aspect was especially dramatic, for most of the artists featured in the 1962 show celebrated the relative opacity of mass-produced images—their flatness, their peculiar deadness, their inability to convey the essence of whatever it was they "signed"—at the same time that they delighted (via scrupulous attention to "realistic" detail) in bringing that object close and making it seem as though it was immediately apparent, right there, present in that very room. For example, Robert Indiana de-contextualized the alphabet, in order to accentuate flatness at the very same time that he imbued letters with deep, vibrant hues in his Scrabble-like arrangement of L, O, V, and E. Roy Lichtenstein, for his part, lovingly "reproduced" the grainy, newsprint texture to comic strips at the same time that he presented, at face value, the stunningly vapid "crying beauties" populating them. But the true star of that show was Andy Warhol, who had hung some paintings of tin cans in a corner.

Warhol had gotten his start as an illustrator in the employ of Bonwit Teller. He had a whimsical eye and built-in fondness for old-world calligraphy mixed well with quirky line drawings of leather shoes, green apples, and butterflies. Hence Warhol began to exhibit professional work at galleries, and when Robert Rauschenberg and Jasper Johns began to use imagery from ads and news tabloids as starting points for serious painting, Warhol realized that his experience as a commercial artist had, curiously, put him in a good position to make his own run at the pressing aesthetic issues of the day. For a while he toyed, like Rauschenberg, with instantly recognizable comic-strip characters and the various kinds of lettering employed by comic-strip creators. But he didn't really hit his stride until, one day, he found himself appraising a drawing he'd made of a can of Campbell's Soup. Warhol had copied the object before him so well that the can in his picture was almost more real than the can on the table. Indeed, it appeared to be *more* real, for now the can positively shimmered with the kind of there-ness that comes with the illusion of complete transparency (zero mediation) and total access. "BOOM!" Warhol was off and running. Elvis posing with a six gun, Marilyn, S&H Green Stamps, two hundred cans of Tomato Soup—from 1962 onwards, viewers of Warhol's work were treated to a kind of orgy built on perfectly achieved copies.

And then, starting just a year or two after the Januis show, Warhol began inviting viewers to more conventional orgies in Warhol-directed films like *Blowjob* (1964), *Blue Movie* (1968), and *My Hustler* (1968).

Thanks to movies like these, of course, a lot of people began to dismiss Warhol as a prankster who had worn out his welcome. In fact, though, Warhol's pornographic movies were the natural outgrowth of his earlier work with soup cans. Indeed, they cemented his position as an artist rather than destroyed it, for now Warhol was making the implications of New Realism clear. What, after all, was the point to his movies? The point—and it was, in retrospect, a very clear point as the sex itself was far from exciting—was that acting is just as superfluous, when push really comes to shove, as painting. The footage in *Blue Movie* was "real." It was (like a silkscreen) stenciled off actual events, and given that this particular emphasis demonstrably commanded attention in ways that traditional emphases did not, Warhol was also arguing that footage resulting from such an emphasis rightfully supplanted less immediately interesting "stories" that had been invented to convey truths not available to real-time witnesses of ordinary life. Was this a good thing or a bad thing? Warhol, I feel sure, did not presume to know. Instead, he simply knew—a little before the rest of us—that our culture had changed. Thanks to his experience as a practicing communicant at St. John Chrysostom Byzantine Catholic Church in Pittsburgh, and then (throughout his adult life) as an abstaining communicant at St. Vincent de Ferrer Church in Manhattan, Warhol understood genuinely word-based culture. It was a given, for him, that ordinary experience was ably known through the mediatory presence of a sign that was different from the thing one was proposing to "know"; therefore, when that bias in favor of logos-based art began to dim in the culture at large, Warhol noticed.

Consider the current-day "hyper-real" movement, which is championed by the computer-graphics industry and driven by a confirmed consumer preference for instantly recognizable, visually certain "signs" regardless of whether or not these signs truly link up with the things they allegedly represent. Think touched-up photos of dewy cans of Coke with clearly defined beads of moisture on aluminum skin. Think Mickey Mouse on Main Street at Disneyland USA. Think green-ness alternating with yellow-ness in a British Petroleum "sun" flower. In each of these instances, the criteria for reality and ensuing convincement have ceased to have any relation to referents outside the zone of signs. Rather, the criteria have become exactitude of detail, inherent desirability, inner coherence, and compatibility with other, similarly unmoored "signs." Hence fantasy and manufactured advertising images both qualify, now, as "reality." Does anybody know where this movement will wind up? I sure don't, and I suspect it would be wise to never try to learn.

Or consider "reality TV" and its theatrical equivalents, where the viewer's "charge" comes from the realization (no pun intended) that the drama unfolding before one's eyes is "really happening." It used to be that we went to the movies or a theatrical production to give ourselves over to an obviously invented fictional world so as to gain a glimpse into the meaning of our ordinary, humdrum lives. Now we go to the movies or the theater to trade that contract in for a different one whereby theatricality gets removed, often by annihilating the difference between audience and actor, to create a passing sense of immediacy.

Big though these developments are, however, they are nothing compared to the widespread acceptance of porn and its consequent enhancement. The stuff is often rocket fuel now; much of it has the power to burn holes in your mind. No doubt this is partly the result of producers' newfound ability to be selective about who to employ as a performer. Chiefly, though, porn now provides a thruster-like boost because, like an uncut drug, it delivers an almost pure form of immediacy. First there's the rush of naïvely defined reality made possible by the knowledge that "actors" on the screen are "really" having sex, and then, once that sensation starts to wear off, there's the intensified "there-ness" of perfectly wordless—e.g., intentionally transparent, therefore unspeakable—knowledge. Is the correct analogy, here, the rapid ignition of fossil fuel that ought, ideally, to be burned or otherwise broken down more slowly? Whether or not that analogy is correct, one can at the very least note that going for broke toward simulation by literally feasting on "things-in-themselves" paradoxically leads viewers to ignore the very same referents that word-signs stubbornly point toward. Indeed, consumers of high-grade porn get to the point where they resent reminders that an "objective" world of, say, potential sexual partners exists, and that development, in turn, causes viewers to mentally replace the dangerous world of people with the plastic, oh-so-subservient world of candied images. Has there ever, anywhere, been a more radical overturning of word-based knowledge? Immediacy, orientation toward fantasy, dividends up front rather than down the line, fixation rather than contemplation—it's all there. Modern-day porn, it turns out, functions as a kind of final cause. It's the end toward which Warhol and Derrida and indeed all advocates of nominalism have tended. When Occam dismissed words as screens, he was pointing toward a wordless reality that would one day morph into porn.

Words, however, are not screens. Just as the real is not positivistic fact or a Kantian projection or a fiction created by a power-wielding subject, so too words are not ciphers that "stand in" for, package, or cloak a referent. Rather, they are first and foremost a kind of parallel creation, a variously complex zone where material vocables are infused with sense in such a way as to re-present the natural world and thereby share in (and convey) the splendor of that world's being. Sure, verbal signification involves "likenesses." One of the chief points, in talking, is to see, over here, the very same thing that we see over there. But words themselves, both as single names and as elaborately constructed clusters of names, have nothing to do with copying or imitating or (as in *trompe l'oeil* painting) inviting an audience to mistake a two-dimensional sign for a three-dimensional referent. Instead, words have to do with communicating presence. Even more incredibly, words accomplish this feat in direct proportion to their obvious difference from the things they represent. Unlike simulation-based enterprises like porn, word-based knowledge depends on there being a remove from the object being apprehended. Eliminate that remove—strive as Warhol did to do an end-run around mediatory agents and "lock in" lurid, triumphantly visual spectacles like Orange Car Crash Ten Times—do that and the whole enterprise collapses.

Who, though, can we turn to besides pre-postmodernist writers, poets, and our best commonsensical selves in an effort to get a firm and detailed grasp of what we're losing as we turn away from word-based knowledge?

The best place to start is by examining the Scholastic tradition that blended Johannine logic with the Platonic theory of Forms successfully enough to invite repudiation by Occam. Thinkers like Bonaventure, Duns Scotus, and Hugh of St. Victor didn't exactly spend their time figuring out whether angels could stand on the head of a pin. On the contrary, they spent their time trying to explain the blazingly evident fact of fleshly existence in all its time-bound specificity. They were interested in things—the force of them, the demands they place on our attention, the way they glow with there-ness. What was a blade of grass? How did it maintain identity through change? Wherefrom the obvious intelligibility and to what extent was that intelligibility proof of a thing's existence? Nowadays only children ask such questions. The rest of us, ostensibly because we are more experienced and less epistemologically naïve, have moved on to map genetic structure and think through the uses of grass. But people living in the medieval era asked about what-ness well into their adult years, owing to their belief that God had in some sense spoken the world into being two times—first during the Genesis event, second during Pentecost. They were inclined to read nature itself as a kind of divine word that "meant" an idea in God's mind. Additionally, they believed that they were in some sense commissioned to share in that creative act by naming objects and knowing them in the light of a human word through which objects continue to "finally" exist. Hence the entire world shimmered with import, in the medieval mind. It was, in that sense, "real." Owing to the average medieval person's bias in favor of verbal signification, nature itself was a burning bush; therefore, medievals spent their entire lives trying to account for the phenomenon.

Well, who needs a burning bush? We have regular ones, and if they don't suffice we can bask in the intensity of the hyper-real! Why, that medium boasts more colors—heck, more (species-free) forms—than Aquinas even dreamed of. Yes?

Truth is, we know we are lying when we talk like this. Moreover we even understand the hugeness of our current predicament as patrons of porn. For it's not just accidental that we are gravitating now toward events like the ones on "reality" TV. On the contrary, it's an indication of our conviction that something valuable called "the real" is eluding our grasp and disappearing even as we speak. The world is growing dark. Juniper twigs, hop petals, flecks of feldspar in granite, the eyes of a tern, even a stripper's fetching legs are fading fast, and therefore we are desperately reaching around for ways to shore up the failing there-ness. We'll give even virtue a try, but the inertial pull toward immediacy is strong, and so far we are powerless to escape it. Hence we push on—toward night.

The Humane Vision of Elmore Leonard

Detroit 2015

I first got acquainted with Elmore "Dutch" Leonard when, quite by chance, I read the first chapter of *Freaky Deaky*, his tightly scripted 1987 take-down of acid-dropping, formerly underground, 1968 Democratic National Convention-derived Weathermen who aspire to put still lethal bomb-making skills to new, considerably more lucrative use after recent stints at Milan and Huron Valley Correctional Facilities just south of Ann Arbor. In the first sentence we learn that Detroit Police Sergeant Chris Mankowski, Crime Lab section, has received a call to remove a possibly activated bomb. Second sentence: "What happened, a guy by the name of Booker, a twenty-five-year-old super-dude twice-convicted felon, was in his jacuzzi when the phone rang." Booker, freshly graduated from street-dealing organizations like "Young Boys Incorporated" and "Pony Down," calls out to his bodyguard, Juicy Mouth, to pick up the phone but Juicy Mouth is absent so Booker has to answer the phone himself. It's his girlfriend. Are you sitting down, she asks. "I *am*," he says, while determinedly settling into a green leather wingback chair that once belonged to one of Detroit's automotive pioneers. "I have sat the fuck down." At which point the girlfriend tells him that by sitting in the chair he has activated a switch that will cause a bomb to go off the instant he stands up.[1]

That kind of opening compels attention, but it isn't until Booker starts berating his would-be savior one page later that Leonard sets the hook. "I been waiting," Booker says. "You know how long I been waiting

1. Leonard, *Novels of the 1980s*, 685.

on you? I don't know where anybody's at. I been calling. You seen Juicy Mouth?" Who is Juicy Mouth, Chris Mankowski wants to know. "Suppose to be guarding my body." Who was the woman on the phone? "Suppose to be in love with me." What'd she tell you? "Say I get up, I'm *blown* up." That's all? "Man, that's final, that's all there is all, nothing else."[2] Yes, but do you believe her, Chris asks. "Asshole, you expect me to stand up and find out?" By the end of that short first chapter, this reader, for one, had committed to finishing the novel.

It turned out to be a big commitment, for upon reading one Leonard novel you tend to want to read another, and it turned out that Leonard had written not just ten or twenty but forty so-called tough guy novels over the course of a career that spanned—this is hard to believe—sixty years. His first novel, *The Bounty Hunters*, came out in 1953, just four years after Ross MacDonald's first Lew Archer detective novel, *The Moving Target*, and three years after pulp fiction veteran John D. MacDonald's crime fiction debut, *The Brass Cupcake*. Yet Leonard's last novel, *Raylan*, featuring the return appearance of a straight-shooting U.S. Marshall from coal country, came out in 2012, a full twenty-five years after the two MacDonald careers had ended. The quality of Leonard's production is of course uneven, and in some of the novels where live-wire zip and zing are absent—works like *The Moonshine War* (1969), *Split Images* (1981), *Cuba Libre* (1998), and *Mr. Paradise* (2004)—Leonard seems not so much to be writing as going through motions and mechanically repeating moves that had worked for him in the past. But, when Leonard is "on," as he was during most of the 1980s and nineties, he is really on—so much so that his writing might at those times fairly be described as dazzlingly electric and superior to the work of his peers.

Wherefrom the difference?

Part of it is that, unlike the novels of hard-boiled fiction master Raymond Chandler, Leonard's novels aren't (ultimately) about the moral ambiguities of crime detection or the pleasures of solving a puzzle. Nor are they (ultimately) about beach-bum expertise or access to friends in high places, as in John D. MacDonald's wonderful private investigator series starring Travis McGee. Trained as Leonard was by writing for pulps like *Dime Western*, Leonard tends to focus instead on moments of truth that people either rise to or flee from, according to varying degrees of valor, imagination, and moral probity. Sometimes the main characters in his novels are cops. Other

2. Leonard, *Novels of the 1980s*, 686–687.

times they are entrepreneurs—think flight attendants who agree to carry cash from an offshore account, or melon-growers trying to beat the weather, or burglars with a business plan, or owners of a company that makes parts for an automotive assembly line. Whatever their line of work, Leonard's characters are ordinary, if underestimated, and this frees Leonard up to luxuriate, if you will, in what Steinbeck called "the poetry of folks talking," be it Chickasaw Charlie Hoke (minor league pitcher) reminiscing (in *Tishomingo Blues*) about striking out Willie McGee in "De-troit" after being sent down to the Mudhens where a pitch that was supposed to curve low and away "bangs letter-high" on a batter; or Harry Arno (bookie) explaining (in *Pronto*) to a sympathetic cop that FBI operatives couldn't possibly determine how much he skims before reporting proceeds to Mob-linked silent partners ("Guy calls up, he says, 'Harry give me the Lions and the Niners twenty times reverse. Bears a nickel. Giants five times, New England ten times *if* the Rams ten. . . .' You're telling me this Bureau guy's people are going to get a read out of that?"[3]); or Zulu and Snow ("jackboys" working for an arms-dealer) trying (in *Rum Punch*) to read directions for a rocket launcher they've just unpacked so as to fend off a SWAT team approaching their door ("Snow said, 'Re- . . . lease. Yeah, it say to release the . . . something. Release the safe-ty. Yeah, that thing right there. Release it.' Zulu said, 'Push it?' Snow said, 'Release the motherfucker however you suppose to. I think, yeah, you push it. The next word it say to aim. . . .'").[4]

But the chief attributes that set Leonard apart are (1) a systematic bias in favor of humor and sunniness as opposed to alienation or cynicism, (2) sustained attention to real-time thinking and what might best be called inwardness-ripening-to-decision, (3) a genius for names, and (4) complete and unadulterated comfort in the company of thieves. Which means: he really *is* the "Dickens of Detroit" his tombstone claims him to be.

Most of us have read *Great Expectations* and so (without too much trouble) can recognize these four traits as Dickensian, but where, in Leonard's case, do the winning qualities come from? In Leonard's case the winning qualities derive from three factors. The first is Leonard's emulation of Hemingway's prose style. Leonard's debt to Hemingway explains to a large extent both Leonard's gift for the sort of plotting that is required if one is to successfully convey instantaneous moments of decision, and, too, Leonard's orientation toward morning rather than night. Without another

3. Leonard, *Pronto*, 12–13.

4. Leonard, *Rum Punch*, 274–275.

determining factor, though, I'm not sure Leonard's attempt to describe the way time widens in moments of instantaneous decision would have been successful, and that supplementary factor is Leonard's experience as a baseball player. (Leonard's high-school classmates nicknamed him Dutch because he aspired to be a pitcher and shared his namesake with Washington Senators knuckleballer Emil "Dutch" Leonard; Elmore was proud enough of this association to get "Dutch" tattooed on his right shoulder in 1946.) You wouldn't think that a background in baseball could be inferred from a Western, but of course it can, for a gun leaving a holster is not unlike the moment when a pitcher reveals, at the very moment a ball is released, the finger placement that will determine the thrown ball's course, and I suspect that transposing a batter's viewpoint so that it can play in a Western gave Leonard the ability to create his signature fifth dimension that permits characters to recognize the arrival of their *kairos*, their moment of truth. And the third important factor contributing to Leonard's artistry? That is Leonard's grounding in the Baltimore Catechism.

Leonard was born and baptized in New Orleans before his father relocated to Detroit after securing a job with General Motors, and Elmore went to daily Mass while attending both Blessed Sacrament Elementary and Middle Schools behind the Cathedral of the Most Blessed Sacrament in downtown Detroit, and then Jesuit-run University of Detroit High School. After serving in the South Pacific during World War II, Leonard enrolled at the University of Detroit to get a B.A. in English, and years later, upon being asked about his training, he said Jesuit instructors had taught him "how to think." Also, Leonard's early Westerns often read, quite literally, like prayer books or catechisms. Acts of contrition and prayers to the Virgin Mary appear regularly as Mexican segundos get into tight spots, and characters like Paul Cable, the *Saber River* protagonist, systematically think through the difference between self-defense and murder before picking up a gun to defend a homestead. Are these religious accents window dressing? Up until 1957 perhaps they were. Starting in the late 1950s, though, Leonard's explicitly Catholic emphases deepen to include the anthropological dimension to Christology, and from that point forward his plots get significantly stronger.

The part of the Christian schema that appears to have intrigued Leonard most, starting in 1959, is the doctrinally sound but often unexplored claim that Christ is a new Adam who, thanks to utter reliance on God the Father, is not ruled by fear of death and consequently never lies.

What would it be like, Leonard appears to be asking, to live like that? The explicitly Catholic aspect to Leonard's developing anthropology reaches formal maturity in *Touch*, the novel about a stigmata-bearing healer that Leonard wrote after quitting alcohol in 1978, but the overall shape of the anthropology is already visible in his early Westerns. "*Ecce homo*," Leonard appears to be saying (in counterpoint to Nietzche) when (in 1961) he names his novel about outcast John Russell *Hombre*. Russell, already an outcast because he is the child of an Apache father and a Caucasian mother, is strange for multiple reasons. He plays, always, for mortal stakes, and he will not, under any circumstance, allow himself to be unjustly put down or used. At the same time, however, if Russell sees someone else suffering an injustice, his default position is to *not* step in to right things in the wronged individual's favor because that would amount to robbing him or her of the chance to fight his or her own battle and so come into his or her own, as a person. If, on the other hand, an individual first shows mettle and then is attacked, Russell will (and does) lay down his own life to ensure that person's continued freedom. Sounds a little like Socrates and perhaps another figure whose name I can't quite remember.

Leonard took a break after writing *Hombre* to solidify finances by writing scripts for *Encylopedia Britannica* films, but directly after selling the movie rights to *Hombre* in 1966, he wrote two other traditional Westerns that advance the anthropological vision mapped out in *Hombre*. In *Valdez is Coming* a temporarily appointed sheriff named Valdez has the temerity to take his job seriously and question whether a man holed up in a cabin with a rifle is as guilty as self-important land barons want him to be, and when the cornered man dies in a firefight with Valdez that was provoked by rifle shots from one of the land barons' hired hands, Valdez makes it his mission to secure modest but real sustenance for the cornered man's Apache widow. Despite an almost literal crucifixion, Valdez of course wins her that sustenance, but that isn't, in itself, the climactic point of the story. The real climax occurs as the land baron's men leave his employ, one by one—owing to growing respect for the rigorously consistent trustworthiness of Valdez' word. And then, in *Forty Lashes Less One*, Leonard sincerely and not ironically references Second Corinthians so as to explain how "strength is made perfect in weakness." Leonard sets things up so the preaching proper comes from the mouth of a well-meaning fool who takes a leave of absence from a ministerial position at Holy Word Church to fill in as warden at Yuma Territorial Prison in southern Arizona, but of course fools in most theatrical productions do turn out to be wise, and in this case the point driven home by the fool is that people are "saved" to the extent that they maintain their status as free persons while performing whatever role is handed them, be that role hardship or joy, and in that way become more themselves.

Dare I say that we have the makings here for the authorial prowess Leonard was later to become famous for, once he had solidified his anthropological vision, devised a way to write in a sunny way about love-making without simultaneously ignoring sex, and begun to focus in a more covertly Christian way on moments when formerly asleep persons wake up? I submit that we do, and I furthermore submit that the moment when it all came together for Leonard occurred when he wrote the admittedly flawed but crucially important "new" Western entitled *The Big Bounce*, which is set in a resort area just north of Detroit on Lake Huron.

The hero of *The Big Bounce* is a petty car thief named Jack Ryan, who surfaces later as a server of court summons in *Unknown Man #89* (1977), the novel Leonard wrote right before *Touch* (1978), and the "bounce" referred to in the title seems at first glance to be the thrill that can be associated with vandalizing property. Over the course of the novel, though, one begins to see that there are also other "bounces" going on, among them the possibility that a girl who introduces Jack to new varieties of breaking and entering may be using Jack for lethal purposes of her own, and the hook is that the biggest bounce of all may come from Jack's ability to recognize that he is being played and then walk through a kind of spiritual door toward goodness that he has glimpsed in a stolid, cigar-smoking justice of the peace who buys Jack a beer, and also in the actions of a priest saying Mass for migrant laborers in a field on the other side of some trees. The Justice doubles as president of the local Chamber of Commerce and his name is Majestyk. To Ryan, "the guy looked like an ex-pro guard hunched over the bar, leaning on his stubby arms . . . talking to the bartender about fishing," and when Ryan claims a nearby stool Majestyk sees that Ryan is a fellow who is destined to appear soon in his courtroom. "So how can you be arrested for vagrancy," he asks. "You ever been picked up for that?" Soon they are drinking Seven Crown and Strohs, and eventually it comes out that a grim reaper claimed Jack's father when the man was only forty-six. "Well, I don't know," Majestyk says. "Sometimes a person just dies." "Yeah, I guess we all have to die," Jack says. "I don't mean that," Majestyk says. "I mean, we're supposed to die. You can't kill yourself but that's what we're here for—to die. Are you Catholic? With your name I mean. . . . You were taught, weren't you?"[5]

I could go on but I think my point is clear. It is this. If we're serious about getting a firm grasp on Elmore Leonard's stupendous accomplishments we should by all means read his best books. That done, however, we should make haste to supplement that effort by acquiring *The Big Bounce* so as to see Leonard at his own professional crossroad. Should we see the movie version of the novel as well? I think not. That film stars Ryan O'Neal, and when Leonard saw it he walked out. "I have now seen the second worst movie ever made," he said, adding: "There has to be one that's worse." One month later he recovered by catching Count Basie with jazz singer Carmen McRae at Whisky-a-Go-Go in Hollywood, but we don't have that option anymore, so we, for our part, need to be more careful.

5. Leonard, *The Big Bounce*, 71–76.

Burning River

Cleveland 2015

When I first emigrated from California to eastern Ohio, the place from which I now write, it seemed as though I had moved to the end of the earth, to a place where some cosmic catastrophe had occurred—catastrophe for which restitution had not yet been made. I had thought I was moving to paradise, to unheralded, therefore secure, farmland that had been only slightly changed since hunters in the Pleistocene stalked wooly mammoths just south of an ice sheet, and, of course, I had, but for a time there (after first arriving) I was just amazed by the scale of the strip mining that had occurred in townships directly to my east and south as the steel industry's need for coal exponentially grew. Hence it was with a sense of recognition and even kinship to discover Belt Publishing's *City Anthology* series, launched in 2013 by Anne Trubek, who had quit her job as a tenured Professor of English, Rhetoric, and Composition at Oberlin College so as to focus more freely on devolution underway in Cleveland after the collapse of that same steel industry just fifteen years after the Cuyahoga River caught fire there in 1969. What has happened here, Trubek aspired to know. How do we identify, much less measure, that which has been lost? And—no less importantly—does such loss provide ballast (and therefore steerage) or doom? These were questions I also was interested in.

There were some differences. Whereas my prompts tended to be rural in character: for *BeltMag* contributors prompts tended to appear in the context of suddenly quieted urban industry. Also, whereas my challenge was to correct inevitably flawed first impressions, the challenge for Belt Publishing has been to reclaim organizing narratives from outsiders who are intent on mining industrial regions for images and/or stories that feed one or another variant of Rust Belt "chic"—be that variant provincial taste, mistake-on-the-lake pessimism, or Mob-related violence. In the end, though, we were looking at the same puzzle, reaching for the same diagnostic tools, and taking the same risks, most notably the risk of overstating the case owing to the breathtaking scale, even the grandeur, of the destruction on view here.

Have we succeeded in our efforts to not overestimate the case?

Belt Publishing surely has, and, thanks to their example and the artists they've introduced me to, I think I can also.

Consider Cleveland Heights jazz critic Harvey Pekar, whose not-so-ironic *American Splendor* comic book (published in 1976) helped to pioneer the graphic novel art form.

"The peddlers, or perrlers, as they used to call themselves, were mostly from Russia and Poland and had heavy 'heccents,'" writes Pekar in the Crumb-illustrated 1987 *American Splendor* strip called *PAY-AYPER-RAGS!* about Yiddish communities on Cleveland's east side. "They used to keep their horses and wagons on 37th St. and Woodland. This was before they got trucks. They used to go to 'Orrorra' (Aurora) to pick up 'metresses,' 'betteries' and copper, go to Turk's delicatessen and brag about how much money they made. They'd say they made twenty-five 'tollars' from the junkyard on East 55th and an extra fifteen on 'schmates' (rags) and paper that they took to the ragshop on 61st and Woodland where it was baled up. They took great pride in ordering chocolate phosphates and corned beef sandwiches for the gang at Turk's." All that, while devoting other strips to disputations on narrative technique wherein Pekar allows himself to talk more directly about, say, "an original, easily identifiable drawing style, notable for its economy, clarity, and strength of line."[1]

That's high quality stuff, every bit as strong as Cleveland native Hart Crane's "Brooklyn Bridge" is, thanks to the depth of the well Pekar is drawing from. Where do its waters come from?

One way to answer this question is simply to note that Cleveland is downstream from Akron, on the Cuyahoga River, and that Cleveland's literary renaissance might well be sustained by Akron to the same extent that its rock 'n' roll heritage, as on view in Alan Freed's 1953 Moondog Coronation Ball and clubs like Speaking in Tongues on West 44th, is sustained by The Black Keys and Terminal Fuzz effect pedals made by Earthquake

1. Pekar, *American Splendor*, 2–3.

Devices. Ultimately, though, answering the question that way would just beg our question, because Akron's industrial base suffered every bit as big a hit as Cleveland's did, in the 1980s, when Goodyear stopped making tires there and other companies headquartered in Akron like Firestone Tire and Rubber, B.F. Goodrich, Mohawk Tire, and the associated Atlantic Foundry closed up shop or moved to a different city under a different name, thus turning Akron, former Rubber Capital of the World, into a de-facto cemetery. And that fact, in turn, means that Akron's cultural life might depend on Cleveland's waters just as much as Cleveland's cultural life might depend on Akron's. No, the real answer to our question is that total loss occasions something new, and our best guide for unlocking that paradoxical puzzle turns out to be yet another artist saluted in Belt Publishing releases—namely, Randall Tiedman.

Tiedman, born in 1949, lived his whole life in North Collinwood on the shore of Lake Erie near the railyards on Cleveland's east side. His home was the top floor of a walk-up duplex with a modest yard that had been purchased by his grandparents, and, except for a short stint as an electrician and a tour of duty in Vietnam, he held just one nine-to-five job for thirty-four years. He was a clerical worker who prepared manuscripts, and his employer—is Tiresias listening?—was the Ohio Library for the Blind on Lakeshore Blvd.

Tiedman was also a boxer. He worked out regularly at the Old Angle Boxing Gym on West 25th below Detroit Avenue, and—being 6'2 and weighing 185 pounds—he trained with Sammy Greggs, who coached heavyweight title contenders. Tiedman's main interest, though, was drawing and painting, and over time he built a modest reputation as an Abstract Expressionist painter of the human body in motion. Then, in 2003, his life changed. He learned he had a heart ailment, and from that point forward he started painting landscapes rather than the human form—usually from the air, looking down and across and toward the north. He used acrylic paint and, working now as a realist who was limited by, but at the same time not entirely beholden to, what Google Earth would show, his vantage point was usually a tad south of the Tremont District on the west side of the Industrial Valley, looking northeast.

In paintings like "St. Neot's Margin," "Night's Speechless Carnival," and "Dove Descending" you see what you might expect to see from such a viewpoint—namely, a wasteland defined by containment ponds, trestles, quieted strip mills, sodium light grids, the superstructure of an interstate highway, sky-blackening smoke spewing out of a still active lantern-like blast furnace now owned by Arcelor-Mittal, and the skyline of downtown Cleveland. Yet you also see other things, most notably flooded stadiums illuminated by the glare of Klieg lights still burning, and water coursing along innumerable interconnecting spillways. Time-wise it's as if a great last wave had just moments before receded. Apocalyptic? Yes. But here's the thing. In virtually every one of these paintings, the viewer's eye can somewhere find rectangular lots that look oddly like fields, and in the distance, on the far side of the city beyond, there is light shining from the clearing-like expanse of a usually white Lake Erie.

Tiedman once said that he tended to think of his paintings as pictorial equivalents of a sound that might best be described as "horns, scattering," and that seems pretty close to the mark. Viewers are almost always left wondering whether this is a new world they are looking at, or an old one, when viewing Tiedman's landscapes, and the wonder is that viewers tend in the main to think, "new."

As we do when reading former US Poet Laureate Rita Dove's story in Belt Publishing's *Akron Anthology* about baton-twirling majorettes who serenely and effortlessly lead marching bands along parade routes that lead from the past to the future. How in the world do they handle that role? According to Ms. Dove, it's easy: "Once you send the baton spinning skyward, calmly released from the upturned palm, all you have to do is wait, gauging the instant when it will return to waist level, then reach out and pluck it out of the air, like a flower."[2]

Wow. What does one do after reading *that*? There's only one thing one can do, and that is to take young Cleveland poet Dave Lucas' advice and go tell it on the mountain that the Cuyahoga is still burning.[3]

2. Dove, *Cleveland Anthology*, 122.

3. Lucas, *Weather*, 15.

Things Have Changed

Hanover Ridge 2016

Pete Hamill, the street-educated newspaperman whose most important claim to fame is outrage at the Walter O'Malley-orchestrated decampment of the Brooklyn Trolley Dodgers ("Dem Bums") to Los Angeles in 1957, learned to write by attending Holy Name of Jesus Grammar School in Brooklyn as a kid and dropping out of high-school at age fifteen to apprentice as a sheet metal worker. Therefore when Hamill speaks people tend to listen, and though people usually find themselves listening to a memoir, novel, screenplay, or New York Post column when they do this listening, I must admit that the piece I return to most often is the set of liner notes written by Hamill in 1974 for Bob Dylan's album, *Blood on the Tracks*, where Hamill claimed that though the madness of 1968 had felled the Weather Underground and sent many if not most once honorable men and women into "a past that never was," Dylan had, confoundedly, "survived." That is to say, he had found a way to continue writing "allusive" songs through which, by "leaving things out," he "allows us the grand privilege of creating along with him" even though he had, himself, fronted at least some of that madness by going electric at the Newport Folk Festival in July 1965 and thereby risked his status as a practioner of, in Hamill's words, "troubador traveling art."

Born as I was in 1954 rather than 1935 like Hamill was, I'm inclined to see Dylan as a musician who has more in common with Chuck Berry and Buddy Holly than François Villon, but I concede Hamill's point about how the allusive aspect to Dylan's music allows it to serve as the soundtrack, if you will, of our innermost lives.

Take "Subterranean Homesick Blues," where the puns just keep breaking like water bubbling up from some inexhaustible font. That song was so brilliant, lyrically and beat-wise, that it literally stopped the fledgling rock movement in its tracks when, after being released as a single in March 1965, the whole world starting rapping it. This, after a so-called political period when Dylan released Woody Guthrie-inspired but previously unimaginable songs like "A Hard Rain's A-Gonna Fall." And to follow that up just five months later with *Highway 61 Revisited*, the thoroughly blues-based album on which Dylan is backed by Al Kooper on organ and Mike Bloomfield on electric guitar, almost defies belief. That album kicked open a door in everybody's mind let alone Bruce Springsteen's thanks in no small part to the use of a cop whistle to announce, as it were, the extent of the mayhem about to ensue as Dylan sets up to parse Genesis 22, the biblical passage where, to use street talk, God tells Abe to *kill me a son*. That's the exact same passage that Kierkegaard wrestled with before putting together his first big book, *Fear and Trembling*, so maybe what's on view here is simply the continuing importance of stumbling blocks when creating a hit, but talent does matter and Dylan's take on Abe's predicament turns out to be every bit as joyous as Kierkegaard's when Abe, confounded, figures God must be joking and God says no. *What*? we all, in unison, say. Then off the guitars go—wheels one way, car the other, brake pedal forever out of reach.

Back though to Hamill's chief point, which was that Dylan had "survived" and, to that extent, put us in his debt. What, exactly, did Hamill mean by that? Given the extent to which Dylan's career was at risk after a motorcyle accident, a decision to stop touring so as to raise a family, and, not least, releasing *Self-Portrait*, a double album that covered other people's songs rather than his own, the appearance of *Blood on the Tracks* was certainly remarkable. How, though, does that put us in Dylan's debt? The answer is simple: Dylan had re-invented himself to the point where he could continue to "give us voice."

That's a key point, well worth noting back in 1974 but even more worth noting now, given that the reinvention Hamill celebrated turns out to have been only the fourth of what turned out to be *eight* different times when Dylan ran out of gas and needed to reinvent himself if he was to continue performing.

First there was, as discussed, the Dylan we met on *The Free Wheelin' Bob Dylan*, *The Times They Are a Changing*, and *Another Side of Bob Dylan* released in 1963 and 1964—the Dylan who opened our eyes to the prospect of hard rain falling during the Cuban missile crisis, let alone yearn for a loved one in a north country fair. That particular Dylan was created out of thin air by Robert Zimmerman, a University of Minnesota student from a middle class home in Hibbing, Minnesota. Second, there was the Dylan we met on *Bringing it All Back Home*, *Highway 61 Revisited*, and *Blonde on Blonde*—the 1965–1966 stellar run that included "Absolutely Sweet Marie", "Like a Rolling Stone," "Leopard Skin Pillbox Hat," and "Stuck Inside of Mobile with the Memphis Blues Again" in addition to "Highway 61 Revisited." And, third, there was the decidedly not ironic, clear-voiced, country-rock pioneering Dylan that we met on *Nashville Skyline* ("To be Alone With You"), released in 1967.

Which brings us to the reinvention heralded by Hamill—the one that gave us "Tangled Up in Blue" as well as "Sara," the achingly slow 1976 tribute to his former wife in which we are invited to picture children running to the water "their buckets to fill."

What are the other four reinventions?

First, starting in 1979 after poor reviews of *Street Legal* and *Live at Budokan*, there was the Dylan we met on *Slow Train Coming* and *Saved*, the Christian witness guy who, powered as he was by gospel singers good enough to raise the dead, convincingly invited his audience to "testify," thereby alienating large portions of that same audience every bit as well as he did when he went electric at the Newport Folk Festival fourteen years earlier. Strong stuff. "Gotta Serve Somebody" is every bit as listenable now as it was in 1979, but Dylan's third preacher-man release, *Shot of Love* (1981), didn't have the same magic, and by 1983 he was ripe for yet another reinvention.

That one (reinvention number six) came quickly and (I suspect) easily, given that Dyan's Jewish roots were as pronounced as his Christian leanings. The name of the album introducing Dylan this time around was *Infidels*, and, given the boldness of its reflections on America as a false New Jerusalem, and Israel as a neighborhood bully, the record turned out to be every bit as provocative as its title suggested.

After that high water mark Dylan drifted again, this time by experimenting with mechanized drum beats all the rage in the music industry after the stratospheric success of ZZ Top on his 1985 album, *Empire*

Burlesque, and then trying to recover from that experiment on *Knocked Out Loaded* (1986) and *Down in the Groove* (1988). He found a momentary reprieve by releasing *Oh Mercy* (1989) where wit and a crisply fast, bongo-like beat are offset by a guitar lines finding their way through murky, swamp-like air, but just a year later he was again adrift at the very same time that (and perhaps because) he was, in effect, crowned as the artist who had incontestably "given us voice" when artists as diverse as Johnny Cash, Roseanne Carter, Stevie Wonder, The Clancy Brothers, Willie Nelson, George Harrison, and, most spectacularly, Lou Reed of the Velvet Underground gathered at Madison Square Garden to sing Dylan songs on the thirtieth anniversary of his arrival in New York. Who could write anything new after an event like that? The odds against walking out of a mausoleum are pretty good. Yet, Dylan beat those odds—first by releasing *Time out of Mind* in 1997 (the album constituting reinvention number seven)—and then, starting in 2001, (here comes reinvention number eight) three more albums (*Modern Times*, *Love and Theft*, and *Tempest)* over the course of eleven years that, together, comprise a run every bit as good as the one he completed between 1965 and 1966.

As I can attest, having seen Dylan bring down the house with versions of "Summer Days" off *Love and Theft* in Berkeley and "Thunder on the Mountain" off *Modern Times* in Cleveland after earlier seeing Dylan perform "Like A Rolling Stone" with The Band in Boston in 1974, and front The Rolling Thunder Revue in Bangor, Maine in 1975.

How did Dylan accomplish this feat? The most sensible answer is probably the safest one—namely, that he was backed in both eras by superbly gifted musicians. In 1965, when *Highway 61* was recorded and performed, Mike Bloomfield, Al Kooper, Bobby Gregg, and Harvey Brooks comprised "the band," and a year later, when it came time to tour England, the Hawks (Robbie Robertson, Levon Helm, Rick Danko, Richard Manuel, and Garth Hudson) comprised "the band" long enough to pirate this latter term when they began to record on their own. Excellent as those artists were, however, it is the musicians who have backed Dylan during his most recent run—Tony Garnier (from St. Paul, Minnesota) on bass, Stu Kimball on guitar, Donnie Herron (from Steubenville, Ohio!) on pedal steel and George Recelli on drums—who will be remembered as Dylan's best band.

That established, I must confess that the explanation I default to, when it comes to explaining how Dylan reinvented himself so successfully in 2001, is that gravitational pull exerted by Pittsburgh and points immediately west (i.e., the secret capital of the United States, as detailed in my last book) made it *impossible* for the producer and director of the fine 2001 film *Wonder Boys* to even *think* of choosing an alternative location for the film, thereby occasioning "Things Have Changed," the song Bob Dylan wrote for the movie that earned him a Grammy and not only launched him into his latest reinvention thanks to upbeat pacing, dark humor, and a plotline that unfolds rather like a conjuror's trick devised by a magician pulling rabbits out of a hat. In addition, it sustained his productive powers thanks to an infinitely variable musical structure that enabled the creation of "Soon After Midnight" with its restful cymbal brushwork as well as "Early Roman Kings," a song featuring a beat so dangerous that you can't help but keep your fingers crossed, while listening.

But here's the deal. (Which is to say, the reason I picked up a pen this morning to start this essay-like escapade.) Dylan's latest, confirmedly stellar run appears, now, to be *over*. Rather than hearing "Dusquene Whistle" and "Pay in Blood" when you go to a Dylan concert these days, you'll hear covers of Sinatra singing "Polka Dots and Moonbeams," "I'm a Fool to Want You," and "The Night We Called it a Day." This, at a time when civilizational ground under our feet is shifting again, as Donald Trump's ability to effectively dispatch the two-decades-old, Bush-dominated Republican right has decisively made clear. Dylan says he's releasing covers of these songs in order to "uncover" American classics made famous by Sinatra, and, who knows, maybe Dylan is, but to me the release of *Shadows in the Night* and *Fallen Angels* is eerily reminiscent of the aforementioned double-album *Self Portrait*, released in 1970.

Will he break out of this mode like he did in 1974 when he recorded *Blood on the Tracks*, the album that so cheered Hamill?

Let us hope Dylan does, for we need to be riding a mail train with him again out on Highway 61 where God wanted that killing done so as to be steeped in his genuinely American version of the Judeo-Christian West when we meet the challenges facing us and thereby fulfill our duty as citizens. Each of us will no doubt have differing opinions regarding which kinds of songs would best address our needs, but I'm confident we will all of us recognize them when they arrive. As those of us in the audience did on July 14, 2007 when Dylan played Cleveland at an outdoor arena on the west bank of the Cuyahoga River under downtown office towers looming to the east. It was a spectacular concert, far and away the best I've seen, with a well-nigh perfect set list featuring "Cat's in the Well" and "Watching the River Flow" as well as "My Back Pages," "Things Have Changed," and "Highway 61 Revisited." But the thing that struck me most was the sight of crewmen leaning on the rail to listen—delightedly!—as the (huge) lake freighter they were manning passed by at the slowest possible speed, just thirty feet offshore.

The name of that freighter? *American Republic.*

Ishmael's Real Name Was Jonah

Hanover Ridge 2020

Like any other card-carrying American I have long believed that Melville wrote one great book and, quite naturally, no others. After all, *Moby Dick* is—unquestionably if improbably—the one American novel against which all others can't help but be measured, given the extent to which, through the use of an alienated workingman as a narrator, enough sea-room is provided to enable readers to live without fear of death and within view of polar citadels from which a white whale can and does glide forth like "a snow hill in air." Tragic architecture, sterling prose, mystical insight, mischievous humor, sustained attention to human character under stress, seemingly antiquarian disquisitions that are ultimately philosophical, steadily increasing narrative suspense—the book's got it all, and as if that distinction isn't enough the book also features prophetic vision regarding America's role on the world stage that is every bit as strong and maybe even stronger than Tocqueville's. How would it be possible for an artist to accomplish more? Unlike most writers, Melville crossed a finish line upon delivering *Moby Dick*, and if the entirety of his production after that point turned out to be a relatively minor drift toward grace notes like *Bartleby the Scrivener* and *Billy Budd, Foretopman*, well, those are the wages for accomplishing something miraculous as a thirty-one-year old.

Imagine, then, my surprise when I chanced to read (in quick succession) *The Confidence Man*, *Pierre*, and *Clarel*, each of which compel attention to the same degree that *Moby Dick* does.

Confidence Man, written in 1856 and set on a Mississippi riverboat carrying passengers to and from St Louis, stars a con artist who creates eight different masks to bilk eight different marks, and the book's appeal lies in the skill with which the con-man gets hearers to entrust to him the entirety of whatever sum they have resolved, quite intentionally, to protect. At one point the confidence man appears as a coal agent selling undervalued stock, at another as a widower requesting aid for Seminole Indians, but most of the time (and especially on those occasions when it is necessary to out-duel fellow operators) the con artist appears as a cigar-smoking, brandy-quickened "cosmopolitan" who bears not a little resemblance to Melville himself, and here the plot thickens some—first because Melville was in grave need of money while writing *Confidence Man*, second because the novel functions, ultimately, as a sharp and highly suggestive depiction of the American tendency to mistake Progress and affluence for Divine Providence. Note too that Melville's swindler character shows up at Easter. In short, *Confidence Man* proved to be a wonderfully entertaining read, so upon finishing it I quickly ordered a copy of *Pierre* (the book Melville wrote in 1852, after finishing *Moby Dick*) to see what else I may have missed.

Goodness. Here too I found myself carried along by artistry that I was beginning to think of as an ever-renewing force. True, there are Gothic aspects to the book that are on one level absurd. On other levels, though, the book is carefully dialed in, for *Pierre* is at root a masterfully patient take on the ways in which a happy man can, quick as a minute-gun salute, dig his own grave. The book has a headlong tilt to it, and there are hilarious supporting scenes where our hero is "packed in the mail for St Petersburg" so that he can survive a day's work as an aspiring writer in an unheated Manhattan tenement. But the true marvel is the weight awarded to forests and horsemanship and butlers at an imaginary ancestral home dubbed "Saddle Meadows."

And that's before even getting to *Clarel*, the eighteen-thousand-line epic poem Melville wrote between 1866 and 1876 while working as a customs agent out of a dockside shack near the railyards at the top of Manhattan's meat-packing district.

Clarel is loosely based on a trip Melville took to the Holy Land in 1857 after finishing *Confidence Man*, and (in a subtitle) Melville calls his long poem a "pilgrimage," which of course it is. Lest one think, however, that the book is about a search for faith, one should quickly add that, first and foremost, *Clarel* is about a pilgrimage in the same way that Chaucer's

Canterbury Tales is about a pilgrimage. In other words, it is a book about tourists who *talk* in entertaining ways for extended periods of time while travelling, which in Melville's case means journeying between Jerusalem, the Dead Sea, and a cliffside Greek Orthodox monastery known as Mar Saba. The book's got eight chief characters: (1) young divinity student Clarel, the protagonist from whose mostly receptive point of view the story is told; (2) his friend Nehemiah, a tract-dispensing, self-appointed protector of Clarel who is convinced that Jesus' Second Coming is imminent; (3) Margoth, a Jewish geologist who is convinced that science, properly followed, will explain away miracles and end the need for all creeds save those accompanying the empirical method; (4) Mortmain, a disillusioned revolutionary who fought in 1848 for the Second French Republic; (5) Derwent, a hearty, hale and thoroughly progressive Anglican priest; (6) Rolfe, a wanderer very much like Melville himself who is "given to study" but inclined to "supplement" Plato with "daedal life in boats and tents"; (7) Vine, a writer modeled on Nathaniel Hawthorne whose eyes are "opulent with withheld replies"; and (8) Ungar, a Native American cavalry officer with "shoulders lithe" and "forest eyes" who is descended, in part, from Maryland Catholics. Needless to say, the topics being discussed in this book matter, and, no less importantly, the characters are drawn in such a way that the reader begins to care, much, about what happens to each of them. As for descriptions of the Holy Land proper, here too Melville succeeds, for he conveys the goodness of wells and "the *ave* of the vesper-doves" every bit as aptly as he presents stony silence and night skies where "stars like silver nail-heads gleam."

Why hadn't I known about these books? Had I been asleep in English class? Wherefrom my mistaken notion that, outside of *Billy Budd*, Melville had written nothing of real consequence after completing *Moby Dick*?

After placing *Clarel* on a shelf where I keep treasured books, I purchased a copy of Raymond Weaver's *Herman Melville: Mariner and Mystic*, published in 1921, and F.O. Matthiessen's *American Renaissance: Art and Expression in the Age of Emerson and Whitman*, published in 1941. It was Weaver who first established Melville's greatness, after ordinary readers almost everywhere had thrown *Moby Dick* to the wayside upon realizing that Ahab's hunt for a white whale was not exactly the simple Polynesian adventure *Typee* had led them to expect, and it was Matthiessen who had most successfully ratified Weaver's claims by placing Melville in a pantheon whose only other occupants were Emerson, Thoreau, Whitman and

Hawthorne. Hence I wanted to learn what these two critics, especially, made of Melville's later work, and after familiarizing myself with Weaver's and Matthiessen's theses I performed a crosscheck of sorts by reading three other studies—Randall Jarrell's 1953 salute to Melville's skills as a poet in *Poetry and the Age*, John Updike's 1982 assessment of Melville's career in *The New Yorker*, and Andrew Delbanco's more recent and no less praised biography, *Melville: His World and Work* (2005). Verdict? I had not been sleeping during English class, and I have not, since that time, been on Mars. Weaver devoted just two out of eight chapters to the entirety of Melville's career after the commercial failure of *Pierre*, and lest anyone miss his point Weaver titled those two chapters "The Great Refusal" and "The Long Quietus." Matthiessen, for his part, called Weaver to task for not paying enough attention to *Israel Potter* (which directly followed *Pierre*), but after that slap on the wrist Matthiessen turned around and devoted just two out of one hundred Melville-oriented pages to *Clarel*. Jarrell, upon close reading, cleverly walked *back* his claim that Melville was as good a poet as Whitman was, Updike considered *Billy Budd* a "return to form," and—Delbanco? This biographer/critic teaches at Columbia University, so maybe he was unwittingly channeling Weaver, but regardless of whether or not there are extenuating factors at work it cannot be denied that this fine critic agrees with the Weaver/Matthiessen interpretation to the point where he actually follows suit—devoting just four pages to *Confidence Man* and (in an attempt to explain how Melville "deliberately hobbled his muse") barely twice that to *Clarel*.

What explains this disjunct? How can so many able readers see in the bulk of Melville's post-*Moby Dick* production a slow and perhaps even intentional drift toward mediocrity and incomprehensibility when the actual works appearing over the course of this purportedly aimless and increasingly bitter period are so engaging?

There are three possible answers to this question: (1) I could be misjudging the quality of Melville's post-*Moby Dick* offerings by overestimating their worth, (2) Weaver, Matthiessen, Updike, and Delbanco could be misjudging the quality of Melville's post-Moby Dick offerings by underestimating their worth, or (3) all of us could be judging *well* on the basis of interpretive paradigms that turn out to be incommensurable. Given the (to me) plain-as-day excellence of Melville's middle and late-period textual records, on the one hand, and the (to me) plain-as-day excellence of Matthiessen's, Updike's, and Delbanco's critiquing skills, on the other, I think the correct answer is the last one, and that the appearance of anomalous results after analyses of the same set of texts is a sign that Melville Studies, so called, may be ripe for the kind of paradigm shift that occurs in scientific revolutions. For that to happen, of course, there would have to be some other paradigm that simplifies reigning explanations of greatness to the point where accuracy is improved. What, then, would be the blindspot that, once grasped, would enable Matthiessen and company to see what I through no merit of my own have chanced to see? It comes down to just one small detail that, so far, has been outside the purview of the critics who have worked hardest to celebrate Melville's achievements: Melville wrote, always, from (and for) a decidedly Christian point of view.

Most of us tend to think that because Melville preferred the company of a cannibal to a drunken Christian and then dared to skewer hierarchical religion through the use of scandalous double-entendres, he essentially parted ways with, to some extent even declared war on, the church-going options that he inherited from his Dutch Calvinist mother. And this assumption is, in a strictly considered way, correct—or at least no less correct than our matching assumption that by relentlessly focusing on the existence of evil, Melville parted ways with, and to some extent even declared war on, the Bostonian, Christ Church Unitarianism that he inherited from his father. Thus it makes a kind of sense that the currently reigning Melville Studies paradigm should have taken hold, and though it makes less sense that we might forget the way in which Melville's alter ego Ishmael predicated his "neither believer nor infidel" motto on the ability to keep "doubts of all things earthly and intuitions of some things heavenly" squarely in view, even that potential forgetfulness makes sense when one factors in the handicap we all now suffer from thanks to the surrender of culture to technology, and the Enlightenment-derived privatization of religion.

The problem is that by committing to the Weaver paradigm we have crippled our ability to see what Melville was actually doing as he followed through on insights gleaned while writing *Moby Dick*, and nowhere is this handicap more clearly on view than in the tortured aspect to Weaver-generated appraisals of *Confidence Man* and *Clarel*.

Despite clear signals from Melville that *Confidence Man* is, ultimately, a reflection on the extent to which there might be an ontological basis to truth which Americans in particular are called to either defend or betray, Delbanco argued in his biography that *Confidence Man* is essentially "a postmodern work in which the swindler cannot be distinguished from the swindled."[1] Three years later (after being struck, I suppose, by the way in which Melville's con artist changes identities as quickly as if they were clothes), Robert S. Levine then confirmed Delbanco's take by arguing (in an otherwise fine introduction to *Israel Potter*) that *Confidence Man* is ultimately about "the instability of character." And things don't get any better when Weaver-based critics get around to appraising *Clarel*, a book where essential dramatic highlights include Mortmain (ex-revolutionary) being "astounded into heaven," Rolfe (Melville stand-in) steering by "Mary's mellow star of eventide," and Clarel (student) emerging "like a swimmer rising" from "the last whelming sea" of unspeakable sorrow. To Weaver-based critics and even to Updike, *Clarel* is not about *any* of these things. Instead, it is about a failed search for God. Weaver's pupil Charles Olson even went so far as to claim, in a celebrated study titled *Call Me Ishmael* (1947), that *Clarel* is a "betrayal" of what the Pacific Ocean taught Melville.[2] Talk about a Great Refusal! Seeing as how the Pacific is where, for Melville, the "flood-gates of the wonder-world" opened and (as in a Pentecostal moment) everything started to mean everything else, Olson's assertion is basically laughable. Yet I doubt very much whether other Weaver-aligned critics have laughed at Olson's conclusion.

Ought we not, then, to take a hint from the increasingly ironic aspect to Olson's kind of refusal and ask whether Melville's steadily deepening use of Christian logic might more adequately explain Melville's development as a writer? For Melville didn't just lean toward Christian biases. Rather, he cultivated them—first by spying out the importance of sacramentality, second by developing a homemade "desperado" theology of being that was strong enough to withstand Matthew Arnold's kind of *Dover Beach* doubt, and, thirdly and most provocatively, by declaring de-facto allegiance to Rome.

It was in *Moby Dick* that Melville intuited and explored the importance of sacramentality, and how could he not, given the extent to which the story of Ahab and the whale is steeped in *King Lear*, the play where Shakespeare's Catholic biases are best on view. When a whale is sighted, Queequeg's, Daggoo's and Tashtego's three harpoon boats instantly swing out to dangle over the *Pequod*'s side like "samphire baskets" next to a cliff—a clear reference to Edgar's detailing of Gloucester's imagined predicament in *Lear*. Then Starbuck offers to be a "blank" in Ahab's eye so as to steer

1. Delbanco, *Melville: His Life and Work*, 248–249.

2. Olson, *Call Me Ishmael*, 102–103.

him toward right vision in much the same way that Kent and Edgar offer to be "blanks" in Lear's and Gloucester's eyes. What is wrong with Ahab and why are the renegades federated along his keel in trouble? It comes down to the same thing that Lear is afflicted by before being humbled by a night spent on the heath—to wit, an inability to see the value of *faces* and, by extension, incarnational life. To Ahab and, indeed, to almost all of us to the extent that we are scandalized by the claim that God can only be seen through a material medium, visible phenomena are merely "pasteboard masks" that ought to be removed so we can better see the Being that "hides" behind them, and Ahab becomes infuriated when, after ripping off intermediaries and going for the thing-in-itself, he finds "nothing." Ishmael, by contrast, reflects on the color that appears when "white" light refracts, and from that point forward he starts to recognize the importance of intermediaries like words, the rightness of enfleshment regardless of the suffering entailed, and the duty to resist temptations to transcend our human estate. In the Catskill eagle section of the chapter entitled "The Tryworks," Ishmael's implicitly Christian resistance even becomes a sort of song. Salvation, he says, isn't found by doing an end-run around creaturely status. Rather, it is found by showing up, giving thanks for the (glorious) light of day, and avoiding evil simply by *being present* no matter what comes. "For even if [we] forever fly within the gorge," he explains, "that gorge is in the mountains"—the dimension where things *are*.[3]

After the financial failure of *Moby Dick*, Melville was under considerable pressure from publishers to produce works which would sell as well as the Polynesian travel adventures that first made him famous, and given that he was also in debt and had a family to support, most of the works that Melville wrote between 1851 and 1857 were, quite naturally, about the jail-like aspect to indebtedness and the absurdity of a capable fellow "preferring not" to get a real job upon glimpsing the looming aspect to impending bankruptcy. Yet each of these works also explored other themes, and starting in 1854 with *Israel Potter*, the fictionalized portrait of a soldier who fought in the American Revolution at Bunker Hill before being captured by the British, the essentially religious project that Melville had begun in *Moby Dick* comes once again to the fore. In *Israel Potter* the subject attracting Melville's attention is, mainly, the extent to which America functions as a New Israel—both for the book's hero, who wanders like Moses for forty years in the deserts of England and France while attempting to get home, and, too,

3. Melville, *Moby Dick*, 365–369.

for the rest of us who harbor millennialist expectations in direct proportion to our prosperity. In *Confidence Man* Melville ups the ante by stopping to consider whether collective belief in America as a new Israel could itself favor the arrival of an Antichrist. This is a risky gambit, but Melville meets the challenge by discovering in the occasion an opportunity to showcase truth's ontological basis, and, as well, the (populist) ability of Americans to recognize that basis. "Thou liest," thunders a Missourian backwoodsman upon hearing the con-artist's promotion of a miraculous herbal cure, and when the Missourian's curt statement is followed by unwavering intransigence matched only by a country merchant's stubborn trust in the filtering value of truth's "stony strata,"[4] Melville's entire novel starts to signify in the new and quite salutary dimension that he will just a few years later begin to systematically explore while writing *Clarel*.

Clarel reads like it was written yesterday. The concerns are that current. And I suspect that if those of us who understand and appreciate postmodern predicaments were actually to sample some of this book's more crucial Cantos, we would have a hard time putting the poem down. Here is Rolfe talking to Derwent, after crossing paths with a Dominican priest on the journey to Mar Saba:

> Who's gained by all the sacrifice /of Europe's revolutions? Who? / The Protestant? The Liberal? / I do not think it—not at all: / Rome and the Atheist have gained: / These two shall fight it out—these two; / Protestantism being retained / For base of operations sly / By Atheism.[5]

Or skip ahead to Ungar talking to Rolfe about the New World as the travelers draw near to the stony silence of current-day Bethlehem:

> If be a people. . . let / From any ruling which fore-ran; / Even striving all things to forget / But this—the excellence of man left to himself, his natural bent. . . / And if, in satire of the heaven, / A world, a new world has been given for stage whereon to deploy the event; / If such a people be—well, well, / One hears the kettle-drums of hell.[6]

Interested? Now go back to the Canto at the book's center, where Mortmain dips a hand into the Dead Sea to offer his companions a sip of the

4. Melville, *Confidence Man*, 84.
5. Melville, *Clarel*, 222.
6. Melville, *Clarel*, 458.

"bitter drink" given to "Christ upon the Tree." Nobody takes Mortmain up on his offer. Come, come, he says. Is it "carnal harlotry" you are afraid of, or perhaps John the Baptist's head on a plate? Taking note of everyone's silence, Mortmain quietly points out that evil, at its root, is a lie with the face of truth:

> Things hard to prove: decorum's wile, / Malice discreet, judicious guile; / Good done with ill intent—reversed: / Best deeds designed to serve the worst; / . . . trad[ing] on the coast of crime / Though landing not.[7]

This latter Canto, preceded as it is by a brief warning in which readers are asked to reflect on Thessalonians 2:7 so as to be able to "read aright," is strong enough to make even seasoned readers of Dante gasp, and when we consider also that this Canto is the crowning achievement of an artistic program that was declared and inaugurated in Chapter Nine of *Moby Dick*—at that point we surely ought to gasp again.

Moby Dick's Chapter Nine consists almost entirely of one Father Mapple's send-off sermon for Ishmael, Queequeg, and all the other whale-men gathered at a New Bedford chapel to receive a customary pastor's blessing before heading out to sea aboard the *Pequod*, and the sermon itself is notable, principally, for the way in which it appears to be directed, personally, at Ishmael. The pastor's theme, naturally, is Jonah—the Israelite prophet who is swallowed by a whale upon fleeing God's commands—but barely a third of the way through the sermon Ishmael, the "cap-and-ball" guy who has just told us that he signed up to avoid knocking people's hats off, starts to squirm in his seat. Look at him, Fr. Mapple seems to be saying. "Plainly he's a fugitive! No baggage, not a hatbox, valise or carpet bag." We laugh, of course. How could we not, given the glee with which Fr. Mapple spins his yarn. Now, though, we can see that Melville too was laughing, because Fr. Mapple, it turns out, was describing Melville the writer every bit as well as he was describing Ishmael. Hawthorne noted that when Melville stopped in Liverpool to visit during his trip to the Holy Land in 1856, he travelled every bit as lightly as Ishmael did, and now that we can read the entirety of Melville's work in the key Melville actually wrote it in, we should also be able to see that by telling the story of Jonah dragged down into the cave of the dead where "oozy weeds about us twist," Melville was in effect pledging to do as Fr. Mapple claims Jonah was instructed to do. "And what was

7. Melville, *Clarel*, 250–251.

that, shipmates?" asks Fr. Mapple, rhetorically, at his sermon's climax. "To preach the Truth to the face of Falsehood. That was it!"[8]

The surprise is that Melville actually honored this pledge.

8. Melville, *Moby Dick*, 46.

Weather Advisory

Steubenville 2021

Let me see if I can get this right. One and a half years ago, the American people and American-based multinational corporations naïvely or not so naïvely accepted the warnings of the U.S. Centers for Disease Control that, owing to the arrival of COVID-19, hospitals would soon be overwhelmed nationwide if we didn't cancel or close sporting events, churches, restaurants, bars, theatrical productions, schools, and even parks to public use, thereby enabling a series of lockdowns that punished lower-middle-class households while generating handsome returns for owners of stocks that had been purchased with money generated by outsourcing factory work that formerly sustained neighborhoods in which lower-middle-class citizens lived. Next, George Floyd's murder by Minneapolis police provoked calls from affluent white people who live in suburban or upscale neighborhoods to defund entire police departments at the exact same time police were most needed by people of every color who live in inner-city neighborhoods where riots broke out in response to Floyd's killing. And then, after statues of Confederate generals Stonewall Jackson and Robert E. Lee were toppled owing to the belief that, unlike similarly racist Union counterparts, these generals had committed treason by fighting for the South in a Civil War that was fought, at least partially, to determine which side was guilty of treason, the Civil War erupted all over again—this time to reinstitute skin color rather than the dignity of the human person as our guiding first principle.

Dizzying year.

And that's before mentioning other significant 2020 events like the metaphysical reach of the U.S. Supreme Court's *Bostock* decision, Turkey's occupation of the Hagia Sophia via eminent domain, and Donald Trump's near victory in a presidential contest that had been rigged by *The New York Times*, China, the entire Democratic leadership, old-school Republicans, Trump's personal failings, the FBI, and almost *all* major corporations to ensure that he lose.

Big as these events have been, however, I have begun to think of their sum total as a prelude to a different, possibly more fearful event still to come. It is possible that I am wrong in this assessment, and indeed I hope that I am. But given the robust energies on view at a New Polity conference on "Founding the Christian Society" that I attended this spring in the former mill town of Steubenville, Ohio, I suspect that my assessment can serve as a reasonable betting line.

What are those energies and what might they mean? Succinctly put, they are energies that bear an uncanny resemblance to ones that surfaced in the Weimar Republic during the late 1920s and early 1930s, when Germany's parliamentary democracy was under stress to the same degree that ours is now and intellectuals began searching for a "third way" to provide solutions to problems that socialism and classical liberalism were evidently unable to solve.

When George Mosse, at the University of Wisconsin, put together his now famous list of leanings that coalesced to produce a fascist state, he discerned five key dispositions: exasperation with liberal democracy as a means of effecting change; rejection of a classless society as an ideal; indignation regarding the degree to which vice and global finance plunder the common good; readiness for battlefield sacrifice; and, no less importantly, a longing for feudal ties and an apparently Volkish era when membership in soil-based, self-governing villages mattered more than class or party. Well, that is exactly what was on view at the March 2021 New Polity conference.

This conference was convened on the heels of the September 2019 debate between David French and Sohrab Ahmari at Catholic University of America about recent defeats in the culture wars and a growing consensus among conservatives in general and Catholic conservatives in particular that, far from being neutral regarding the various faith-based groups that are allegedly competing for space in the "public square," liberalism is itself a faith-based project that is actively undermining Christian culture by sundering faith from reason and privatizing religion. Do we really have to accept "drag queen story hour" at our local library? Many think not, and New Polity's chief purpose in convening the conference was to test and evaluate the wisdom and feasibility of a newly minted alternative to liberalism known as "integralism," where thinkers advocate for the integration of church and state rather than their separation. It's a timely proposal and certainly deserving of the attention awarded by conference organizers, given that it helps us to break free of habitual mindsets that could, even now, be hindering right vision. But there was also cause for concern at the conference, because if you had attended you would have recognized all five of Mosse's markers while being treated to assertions that in a state properly aligned to Leonine teaching rulers become good by having to conform their actions to a just end, and paeans to an explicitly Catholic Austrian-Hungarian Empire in which church and state were integrated to the point where subjects allegedly resisted totalitarianism better than German citizens did when Hitler tilted them toward a nationalist Third Reich.

Don't get me wrong. I am not saying integralism itself poses any real danger. Nor am I saying that we could see in this country some version of Nazi ideology that might propel us toward a Final Solution or world conquest. Though we appear to be obsessed by race every bit as much as Germans were, our goal is entitlement rather than liquidation, and, as for world conquest, we have no need for that inasmuch as (for better or worse) our military is already present on every continent thanks to the defeat of Germany, Japan, and, more recently, Iraq. No. What I'm concerned about is the strength of the storm that could occur if ordinary citizens fall prey to the same temptations to which more fanciful integralist theoreticians appear to be falling prey to as they think about whether to chuck civility and reliance on First Amendment rights to the winds and commit to a "third" alternative that may just be merely a different version of the totalitarianism they believe they are fighting.

To be fair to integralists, there are excellent reasons for the discontent driving their hopes. After all, the liberal orders devised by John Locke on one hand, and Rousseau on the other, were themselves predicated on the removal (by Francis Bacon and René Descartes) of perennial philosophy as a civilizational end so as to elevate mechanical philosophy and, ultimately, power itself to rule in that former end's stead. Instead of contemplating that which "is" in and through the Word, we chose, starting in the early fourteenth century, to focus on how a given thing could be used to build ourselves up—if necessary, at Creation's expense—as occurred (definitively) when King Henry VIII seized British monastic lands that had formerly served as a commons. Thus, it would be all but impossible to find, in liberalism's vaunted "neutral" zone, a climate that would positively favor the kind of human flourishing that occurred in the Middle Ages. True, Locke does take time to disassociate state-of-nature freedom from license. But, like Thomas Hobbes, whose thought Locke only apparently opposes, Locke worked, essentially, as an apologist for a collective decision to upend the federated medieval order and, in effect, steal its capital. That's why the garden in which he does his thinking—the so-called "state of nature"—is *empty*.

Therefore, it makes sense that integralists should now advocate for forms of government that are ordered to what's good, true, and beautiful to the same degree that the Church is, so as to avoid and to some extent pre-empt the appearance of "drag queen story hour" at public libraries on the one hand, and the essentially Stalinist ideology that "cancels" dissenters on the other. What *doesn't* make sense—and here we get to the crux of the problem with integralism—is that the "third way" promoted by integralists features a mindset that can be every bit as anti-Christian as the mindset that governs cultural revolutionaries.

This can be discerned two ways.

The first is to notice that woke ideology and maximal integralist solutions both concentrate power at the top. The former does so by substituting social-media sites owned by one or two major corporations for real brick-and-mortar public squares so as to implement the perfect society by tilting algorithms to favor woke thinking the way a casino mechanic might fix a wheel or load dice to disable a run on the house. The latter does so by committing to monarchical government or an administrative state that has been thoroughly infiltrated by Catholics so as to implement the perfect society from above, rather than creating the conditions necessary for justice to grow from the ground up, as it did in the time of the Apostles and, after Constantine and before absolutist states, in the Middle Ages.

And the second way? That is to notice how woke ideologues and integralists both favor coercion as a means of ensuring that persons conform "correctly"—in wokedom's case by identifying dissenting opinions that make progressive people feel "unsafe" and then prescribing cancelation as a means of purifying multicultural free-speech "environments," and in integralism's case by using neo-Scholastic proofs to identify heretical positions and then prescribing fines, incarceration, or death as "pedagogical aids."

What, then, to do?

Given the severity of the political winds that could come our way, I am convinced that Catholic post-liberals, so called, should join hands with (ironically!) the very same people who (only five years ago!) were least inclined to see liberalism as a problem—namely, old-guard conservatives like David French who are aligned with John Courtney Murray's early-1960s proposal that democratic liberalism can support, and not undermine, a Christian culture—and begin advocating for the continued separation of church from state as codified in American founding documents. Though Fr. Murray clearly underestimated liberalism's potential to work as a solvent every bit as much as he overestimated the compatibility of Thomistic and Enlightenment-based definitions of nature, the hope he drew from the American founding was well placed. How could it not be? Thanks to Madison, Jefferson, and, perhaps above all, anti-ratification lobbyists who kept Hamilton in check, protections against tyrannical power that got embedded in our Constitution and Declaration of Independence were substantial, and many of them are still operative.

The First Amendment, in particular, is of inestimable worth, given the protections afforded therein for religious liberty, and though it is almost certain that Jefferson prized the separation of church from state as a means literally to exclude Christian faith-based discourse from legislative deliberations, it is no less true that he aspired to, and in many ways did, secure Anglo-Saxon legacies like the one belonging to the Magna Carta (signed in 1215), thanks to his advocacy of institutional pluralism. In any case, Jefferson's attempt to separate church from state functions today as a crucially important roadblock that could stymie the efforts of would-be theocrats who might soon be hailing now from the Right (thanks to integralism or whatever comes down the pike as its less-academic substitute) in addition to the Left. Indeed, it could stymie theocrats long enough for authentic carriers of the medieval inheritance to build a foundation for whatever new form of Christendom is surely destined to emerge from the bottom up.

Post-liberal Catholics like to point out that the preponderance of iPhones combined with the liberal order's demotion of the "one holy catholic and apostolic church" to a "faith-based group" is demonstrably destroying culture faster than it can be built. And, of course, this is true. But that doesn't mean it's time to head for the hills or retreat to a monastic life that is itself facing serious challenges. On the contrary, it means it's time to take a hint from Jefferson's vision of America as an assortment of "ward republics" and start investing in small towns and inner-city neighborhoods to the point where they become, once again, the genuinely localized economies they used to be. Such areas needn't be overtly Christian in order to prosper. In fact, they probably shouldn't be, given that the time for confessional states has, for all kinds of good reasons, passed. All that's necessary, now, is to boost local economies to the point where town squares and village greens function again as seats of government that allow for and even favor the reinstitution of personhood and reality as organizing principles.

What Tocqueville Couldn't See

Hanover Ridge 2023

I can remember almost to the day the moment when I first glimpsed the technocracy rising in our midst. It occurred in 2022 while my wife and I were journeying to northern Michigan where we have long rented a cabin on a beach for a week, and the events leading to that glimpse remain as vivid for me as, well, Christmas.

We were on Interstate 80 somewhere between Cleveland and Toledo, headed west in a used but well-preserved 2010 Camry, and—already challenged by concrete construction-lane "dividers" that kept twisting us left or right with only inches to spare—who should appear in our rearview mirror but eight spanking-new "blacked-out" Chevrolet pickup trucks traveling at high speed almost bumper-to-bumper with Patriot flags flying, NATO-grade AR-15s stowed discreetly under King Cab seats, and huge, enormously wide spare tires cinched down tight onto cargo beds. Looking forward, I saw with relief that the construction zone was about to end, but the minute we spilled out onto what was, clearly, the middle of a blessedly wide, three-lane highway with shoulders, I discovered that we were in fact on an entrance ramp to yet another bobsled track defined by tractor-trailer trucks belonging to Amazon Prime, UPS, and Marathon Oil on our right, and a now completely revved-up, clearly jubilant line of blacked-out trucks on our left. Were we in a movie? It felt like we were. It felt like we were not just watching but somehow *in* or rather *on* Mad Max's *Fury Road*. Those guys to our left? They were "War Boys," fresh from a raid on blue-state Cleveland. And those trucks belonging to Amazon?

They were "War Rigs," driven (no doubt) by social-justice warrior Charlize Theron or, who knows, maybe even Mad Max himself, aka Tom Hardy, who was done with tyrants and hellbent on backing up Charlize so she could succeed in her effort to redeem "democracy" and restore power to "the people." And we, Lord help us, were *between* the two lines of vehicles, hunkered down about as low as we could get to avoid grappling hooks with cables attached, surely being launched from our left, while whatever rogue War Rig Charlize happened to be driving braked defensively and then suddenly accelerated, thereby creating slip streams that kept us hurtling forward past glimpses of Lake Erie algae blooms and large billboards saying Jesus Saves. For miles. Indeed, it wasn't until we reached the spot on 23 just north of Toledo where you see signs for Huron Correctional Facility that we finally found a way to exit and take a deep breath.

What, I wondered, had been going on back there on Interstate 80 as stop-the-steal, QAnon-fueled Patriots seemingly did battle with social justice warriors? Could that be America? Clearly. Wherefrom, though, the *spirited* aspect to this combat that we all recognize? Is this aspect familiar because, as every newspaper columnist suggests, the American Civil War is about to re-ignite? Apparently so, for safety and distributive justice are non-negotiable first principles for apostles of democracy to the same degree that the freedom to own guns and not be cancelled are non-negotiable first principles for Patriots. As Lincoln famously said, it's got to be "all the one or all the other."

Yet if that is the case, why are the two sides so similar? Why are New Right students, in 2023, setting up tables with flyers promoting "free speech" at Sproul Plaza in Berkeley exactly like New Left students once did in 1962 at the same location? Note too that the Left's tendency to demonize "fascists" on the basis of alleged "nationalism" (starting in 1938 when American progressives flocked to Spain to fight Franco and the Catholic Church), is practically indistinguishable from the Right's tendency to demonize "communism" on the basis of alleged atheism (starting in 1917 when Bolsheviks took power in Russia). Indeed, the two "sides" are so similar that they are almost interchangeable and, in some cases, interchangeable-in-fact, as when, during the Black Lives Matter movement, Blue State progressivists flipped from their former Civil Rights era position and started advocating for the re-institution of skin color as a criterion for judging suitability in a job search.

Say, though, that you conceded the similarity thesis and adopted "magnetic field" (rather than Civil War) as our best interpretive key. How would you explain the occurrence of such a field? What would be its power source, and toward what end would the generated power be directed?

Here the answer (as I learned while studying the puzzle over dinner) came swiftly and surely, for I had only to look at the chart of similarities to understand its shape.

Current-day iterations of progressive and conservative positions tend to generate excitement because they are billed as new, be that iteration the current "woke" critique of FDR's reliance on southern Democratic Jim Crow-oriented political machines to secure a New Deal, or the Trump-inspired National Conservative critique of "theocon" agendas *and* Reaganite economics. Ultimately, though, each of these ascendent political ideologies privileges a strong, massively centralized state so as either to install safetyism or to regulate corporate power in an effort to protect charter schools and parental authority. As did older iterations when we as a country decided to protect ourselves from "fear" via New Deal legislation (as occurred in the FDR era), or contain "communism" via massive military build-ups (as occurred in the early fifties when William Buckley and Brent Bozell controlled the levers of conservative power). No matter which iteration of progressive and conservative positions you look at, you notice that the power of multinational corporations and the centralized state enabling them has either grown or is projected to grow.

Bingo: corroborating evidence indicated that the magnetic field postulated earlier was real. And on that not completely happy but (to me) relatively restful note, my wife and I signaled for our bill, procured two cups of hot China black tea, and (after thanking our very patient waitress) got back on the road.

Somewhere past Bay City, though, right around the spot where the highway climbs, aspens appear, and land tilts north, it struck me that the magnetic field governing conservative and progressive positions appears to be intensifying, inasmuch as constitutional lawyers on both "sides" are now working hard to mine the Fourteenth Amendment's "privileges and immunities" clause in addition to the "due process" and "equal protection" clauses in order to further lock in top-down agendas in the face of potentially hostile state power. This, right as charges of "fascism" and "communism" are increasing. (Even as I was writing this, Robert Reich, former Secretary of

Labor under Clinton, had just published an article in *The Guardian* titled "The Republican Party is Hurtling Toward Fascism.")

Might it not be the case that, ever since WWII and the following Cold War, conservative and progressive interpretations of each other's positions could be accurate and that we ourselves, as a nation, are thereby (through a bi-polar dynamic) fueling the rise of a global totalitarian state?

"'Twas new to me," said Tocqueville, when he first caught a glimpse (in 1839) of the technocracy we were apparently destined to build. After rejecting "tyranny" and "despotism" as appropriate labels, he resorted to describing "an innumerable crowd of like and equal men who revolve on themselves without repose." Looking up as well as forward, he saw "an immense tutelary power . . . which alone takes charge of assuring their enjoyments and watching over their fate." He called that power "absolute, detailed, regular, far-seeing," and he furthermore noted that it "foresees and secures [men's] needs, facilitates their pleasures, conducts their principal affairs, directs their industry, regulates their estates, [and] divides their inheritances." Then comes the punchline: "Each individual allows himself to be attached" precisely because "it is not a man or a class but the people themselves that hold the end of the chain."[1] What would Tocqueville say if he could see what we now see? Would he say "I told you so"? I think not. Instead I submit that the "religious terror" under whose spell Tocqueville professed to be working[2] while writing *Democracy in America* would be deepened. For what we are seeing now is not just tutelage but fraudulence, as new technological advances are sold and positioned as salvific in a Christian sense when in fact they destroy the incarnational underpinning for genuine versions of that same Christian sense.

Artificial intelligence has been around for a while, at least since 1956 when (right as the Cold War was ramping up) Norbert Wiener started to think in terms of teleological "mechanisms," but its growth has increased to the point where observers are starting to predict major social upheaval as more and more jobs currently performed by humans (driving cars, making a jet, even flying one) become automated. Now, however, upheavals are spreading to yet more areas of society owing to the arrival of "generative" intelligence where machines learn from experience and even converse with humans in whatever language we ask them to speak. Witness the arrival of ChatGPT, the online site where many of us have

1. Tocqueville, *Democracy in America*, 662–663.

2. Tocqueville, *Democracy in America*, 6.

already posed relatively complex questions to a "generative pre-trained transformer" and received written replies in which you can discern roughly speculative power if not (yet) the ability to say decisively that one thing is unqualifiedly right or another wrong.

Thanks in no small part to the appearance of a new book co-authored by Henry Kissinger (of all people) about the kinds of security risks embedded in this kind of artificial intelligence, ChatGPT has become a hot issue, and thanks to the entry of Noam Chomsky (Kissinger's former nemesis) into the fray by way of an answering *NYT* op-ed piece ("The False Promise of GPT"), the issue has become hotter still. (In addition to being a linguist of great distinction Chomsky stubbornly advocated for Palestinian interests while Kissinger worked to legitimize Israel's right to maintain control over territory claimed during the 1973 Arab-Israeli War.) Chomsky, not surprisingly, argues that Kissinger and his co-authors overestimate the degree to which generative intelligence is dangerous, arguing that the "amorality, faux science, and linguistic incompetence of these systems" merit "laughter" rather than concern.[3] But so far as I can tell, Kissinger and his co-authors do make one quite valid point, which is that Chat GPT's "answers" regarding the statistical probability of success for one option or another given circumstances too complex for us to grasp will surely outrun our ability to understand those answers. It will be as though a new kind of divine "revelation" is at hand in the face of which signs will have to be taken purely on faith rather than on faith joined to reason.

This, at the very moment when the Catholic Church, the presumed guardian of faith joined to reason, is demonstrably failing in its duty as trustee of that same logic because, vulnerable as it is to the same furious winds that are fueling the displacement of Aristotelian teleological concepts by cybernetics, Vatican II, the Council that formally, finally, and irrevocably positioned faith joined to reason as the Church's theological, philosophical, and liturgical center, is being overshadowed and in some cases *blocked from view* by increasingly clamorous debates between progressives and faux traditionalists, who, together, are reinstituting the very same, ultimately Manichaean dualism that Christianity, by definition, frees us from.

Not a happy state of affairs.

Back to the culture at large though. Surely there are signs out there that things are not as bad as they seem?

3. Chomsky, "The False Promise of Chat GPT."

To consider this question, I decided as a kind of thought experiment to sample representative written works by the best of the conservative Right and progressive Left, and—given that readable liberal theorists (outside of Rawls, who published sixty years ago) turn out to be as rare as conservative-leaning novelists—I decided to focus on Harvard-based political theorist Adrian Vermeule and Manhattan-based novelist Amor Towles, to assess the climates in which conservatives and progressives, respectively, do their thinking.

These are both good writers.

Vermeule almost instantly changed the terms according to which all New Right theorists (and not just integralists) debate and think when he published *Common Good Constitutionalism* (2022). His thesis that the either/or of "living constitutionalism v. originalism" should be retired is persuasive, and his observation that the two schools of thought "comprise a symbiosis of rivalry, exploiting the other as its necessary hate object and fund-raising target"[4] to the point where they are "co-conspiratorial" against "classical tradition," is, to me, incontestable. What, though, does Vermeule mean by classical tradition? According to Vermeule it is the tradition that should be ruling constitutional interpretation in this country, and he defines that tradition as an amalgam of natural law, Anglo-Saxon common law, and a cluster of Roman laws that emerged from 27–23 B.C. during the Roman Imperium as bureaucrats exercised authority that had been delegated to them by the Emperor in such a way as to institutionalize the practice of what the Catholic Church was later to call "subsidiarity." That's a bold thesis no matter how you cut it, but so far as I can tell it can only be cut one way, which is as an occasion for fear—fear that our already massively centralized state will become more so and that the common, Jeffersonian understanding of subsidiarity as locally-owned power granted to kings on condition that kings not behave tyrannically is about to disappear.

As for Towles, he for his part uses powerful and quite winning narrative skills not only to defend the crucial importance of Western Civilization, but also to define aristocracy and associated wealth as earned and in that sense available to all regardless of your standing at birth so long as you refuse to be bought (if you are poor) and are willing to risk all (if you're rich). In other words, Towles' work stands as a rebuke to anyone who claims that progressives have lost access to common sense. Yet you can't help but notice that, ever since the appearance of his entirely

4. Vermeule, *Common Good Constitutionalism*, 12.

convincing *Rules of Civility* in 2011, there has been an increasingly escapist dimension to Towles' work—and I don't just mean that he persists in thinking of America as a meritocracy when to an important extent the accelerating divide between rich and poor in this country now derives from decisions by multinational corporations and their stockholders to outsource manufacturing. I mean that there is now an embalmed aspect to the places and time periods that serve for Towles as settings when he attempts to laud America as "our last best hope." In *The Lincoln Highway*, his most recent book, it's as though government "for, by, and of the people" is preserved rather than re-membered, and, as a result, the book reads like a well-curated exhibit of things that used to be but no longer are. Dare I call it the literary equivalent of a Wes Anderson movie or, even better, Americana music? Often the time-specific riffs that Towles plays to evoke places like Ogalalla, Nebraska, in 1952 with its "motor courts," or Italian East Harlem restaurants in the Bronx where there are "no menus and every table is spoken for," are performed as T. Bone Burnett would perform them—i.e., sharper and more effectively than the artists who first created the riffs that we now think of as names for those places and times, owing to the degree to which the original riffs derived from what was actually heard rather than from what people wanted to hear.

In sum, our predicament appears to be every bit as sobering as it first seemed to be.

Given that the technocracy rising in our midst is already strong enough to enable residency in a world that promises sight for the blind, safe "speech environments," and, most importantly (for those of us who have driven recently from Cleveland to Toledo on Interstate 80), *safe highways*, I have no doubt that Jesus's Sermon on the Mount will, in the future, seem less and less relevant. How, then, can we preserve access to the kingdom Jesus gave his life to establish? So far as I can tell there is still just one way forward, that being to look, with Plato's guidance, at the shadows displayed on our laptop "walls" long enough to discern there the traces—call them shadowgraphs—of an incarnational center's absence, and then, through the negatives that those shadowgraphs in effect are, "see" that same incarnational center clearly enough to induce the existence of a sun and start walking toward the increasingly curious phenomenon known as "daylight."

America's Deposit of Faith

Steubenville 2023

Several months ago, after being invited to give a talk at Bookmarx Books in Steubenville, Ohio, a couple days after July 4, I found myself in an interesting predicament: how to celebrate America as a land of promise without relying on, or having recourse to, standard city-on-a-hill conceits like an allegedly Christian aspect to our founding, or a Constitution built on political principles favoring limited government, or our Lockean commitment to the separation of church and state.

Those are compelling claims, well worth debating, but they are also—as I learned to my dismay while writing a book about eastern Ohio and the trans-Allegheny West—completely untenable. Not because, as post-liberals routinely suggest, we are overly indebted to Lockean anthropology and, to that extent, completely entrapped by liberal terminology however much we may want to escape it. (After all, you can still *read* Plato and, to that extent, think outside the liberal "box" if you want to.) Rather, city-on-a-hill conceits are untenable for three other reasons. First, because our operative power source, the bi-polar energy flow generated by the Second Great Awakening (ca. 1790–1840), bears little to no resemblance to Christianity, strictly considered. (Christianity, founded as it is on belief in the Incarnation, the event whereby "the Word was made flesh," involves a commitment to sacramentality and the integration of nature and grace, but the Pentecostalism that appeared in the upper Ohio Valley in 1801 during the Second Great Awakening depended on maintaining nature and grace as *separate* dimensions so as all the better to taste the differences.) Second, because, thanks to the Civil War, we all steer now by universal suffrage rather than tradition, thereby disenfranchising the dead and the unborn. Third, because the federated polity founded in 1781 by the Second Continental Congress ceased to exist in 1868 thanks to the passage of the Fourteenth Amendment, a piece of legislation that transferred power from the "several states," so called, to the federal government. This made possible the massively centralized state we know today and, eventually, the belittlement of our First Amendment protections, given that the Fourteenth Amendment effectively transferred to the federal government the very same societal capital that the first ten amendments (i.e., the Bill of Rights) were designed to protect.

Witness the imminent elimination of cash economies and the arrival of "social credit scores" that will affect the ability to acquire property or take out a loan. Witness also, and even more importantly, our growing willingness to trade liberty for safety, per terms dictated by Meta, Alphabet, and Amazon.

All that being the case, it seemed unlikely that a way to celebrate America as a land of promise could be found. Nevertheless, there turned out to be a way to meet the challenge.

How? By showcasing the benefits of accelerating interfaith dialogue? Or explaining that the field-tested idea of personhood, already transformative for saints like Dorothy Day, is destined to have a transformative effect on American society at large?

No, for those kinds of advances would not, in themselves, put us in position to defend America as a "land of the free."

The challenge was met, instead, by highlighting one clear, simple, and quite bright fact, which is that Americans are *predisposed* to effectively meet and counter the temptation to trade liberty for security thanks to inherited capital banked on our behalf before the Civil War—capital that functions now rather like a deposit of faith in that it enables and encourages navigation toward the good, the true, and the beautiful.

Depositum fidei: "The body of revealed truth in the Scriptures and sacred tradition." I employ the term somewhat mischievously because America has long had a complicated relationship with Christendom, regularly claiming to be a New Jerusalem when, clearly, it isn't and never was. (The Puritans in Salem, Massachusetts, thought of themselves this way, and the trope only strengthened as our nation expanded westward across the continent and then all the way to the Philippines on the strength of an engineered war with

Spain and Manifest Destiny narratives that allowed us to mine soil, small towns, and traditional cultures worldwide for immediate rather than long-term profit while at the same time destroying access to metaphysical bearings.) In the main, though, I employ the term *depositum fidei* seriously and without irony because in some strange and cosmically paradoxical sense we also, as a people, have a unique ability to see and recognize truth, should we want to, and for the simple reason that, whether we know it or not, our minds have been molded and formed by a body of literary work that enables us to recognize a lie and call it out for what it is.

I refer, of course, to the American Literary Renaissance, an extraordinary burst of artistic energy that ran from about 1837 to 1859 in which Nathaniel Hawthorne, Herman Melville, Henry David Thoreau, Walt Whitman, and Emily Dickinson all found their stride as writers.

Perhaps because he gave so much weight to Ralph Waldo Emerson, F.O. Matthiessen got a few things wrong in his groundbreaking book about the event, *American Renaissance: Art and Expression in the Age of Emerson and Whitman*. The most important is his implied suggestion that artistic energy during the 1850s culminated in Whitman's *Leaves of Grass*, published in 1855. Whitman is, unquestionably, a great poet. How could we not be moved by his descriptions of stevedores unloading ships, hammermen driving spikes to lock in steel rails, and cradles endlessly rocking? "Unscrew the locks from the doors / unscrew the doors themselves from their hinges!" The man almost literally chants democracy into existence by liberating "self" even more thrillingly than Emerson did. "Plumb in the uprights, well-entreatied, braced in the beams . . . . / I and this mystery here we stand."[1]

But the other writers whose works Matthiessen scrutinizes—namely, Thoreau, Hawthorne, and Melville—didn't. Instead of idealizing equality and choice as first principles, these latter authors told cautionary tales about democracy so as to focus all the better on truth. Therefore Matthiessen's book, to an important extent, compromises our ability to see and understand the American Literary Renaissance simply by virtue of its title and the way it is structured. Moreover, Matthiessen's admittedly lengthy discussion of a "metaphysical strain" in the thought of both Thoreau and Melville has more to do with the extent to which they were influenced by seventeenth-century

1. Whitman, *Complete Poetry and Prose*, 28.

metaphysical poets like George Herbert and John Donne than the degree to which they were interested in metaphysics proper.[2]

The bottom line is that some changes are in order if Matthiessen's "American Literature" establishment project is to be brought to lasting fruition, and item #1 should be to redistribute the weights that provide ballast for his summation by concluding the study with Emily Dickinson rather than Whitman. Dickinson merited just one footnote in Matthiessen's 1941 version, but she deserves better given that she channels lightning in addition to simply casting light. Also, she holds her own when standing next to Melville in ways Whitman cannot. But the real benefit to concluding the study with Dickinson is that, after making the change, we find ourselves looking at four mutually supportive "gospels" that are every bit as consistent with one another as are the four Gospels in the New Testament. Everything falls into place, with Hawthorne standing next to Thoreau, Melville, and Dickinson much as John stands next to Mark, Matthew, and Luke. Moreover, these four American "evangelists" support one another to the point where they provide artistic heirs (destined, unwittingly, to be agents of "sacred tradition") with eminently mappable ground to stand on, defend, and argue about.

Which they did.

Robert Frost (poet and writer-in-residence at Middlebury and Amherst Colleges), Ernest Hemingway (newspaperman-turned-novelist), and Wallace Stevens (Hartford-based insurance executive) weren't bishops, but, as writers, they believed things don't become real until written or said. It's why they wrote. Hemingway once remarked, in an interview granted to *Esquire*, that "all good books are alike in that they are truer than if they had really happened," and, different as these three writers were, they would all have approved. All of them turned out to be as committed to Johannine logic as the diminutive, Coptic, working-class St. Athanasius was back in the fourth century, and not a whit less willing to enter a brawl to settle disagreements about how best to articulate that logic.

The conferences Frost, Hemingway, and Stevens attended in the 1930s took place mostly at Hotel Casa Marina in Key West, Florida, rather than in Nicaea, Ephesus, or Chalcedon, but they were equally contentious.[3]

Stevens to Frost in 1935: "Your poems are too academic."

Frost to Stevens: "Your poems are too executive."

2. Matthiessen, *American Renaissance*, 89–97.

3. Schjeldahl, "Insurance Man."

Stevens: "The trouble with you, Robert, is that you write about subjects."

Frost: "The trouble with you, Wallace, is that you write about bric-a-brac."

One year later, with his best poems still not written, Stevens was back, this time telling fellow conferees that Hemingway, already famous the whole world over for simple declarative sentences, was "a sap" and "no real man." Upon learning of the insult, Hemingway showed up, whereupon Stevens (who stood 6' 2 and weighed 220 pounds) took a swing at him and missed. After Hemingway sent Stevens sprawling with two quick punches, Stevens hit Hemingway hard in the jaw while he was taking off his glasses, and, needless to say, Hemingway at that point put Stevens down for the count. Later, Hemingway cheerfully accepted Stevens's apology, and they went their separate ways to write (in Hemingway's case) *For Whom the Bell Tolls* and (in Steven's case) a truly magnificent, century-defining poem called, well, "The Idea of Order at Key West."

What, then, is this ground that Frost, Hemingway, and Stevens were standing on and helping to define? What "deposit of faith" is on view in the scriptures that Hawthorne and the three American "synoptics" created? Quite simply, it is belief in, and deference to, reality.

The renaissance proper begins with the publication in 1850 of *The Scarlet Letter*, Hawthorne's masterpiece about Hester Prynne, the adulteress who is forced to wear a tunic emblazoned with the letter "A" while carrying a child so her hometown can recognize her as a sinner and, accordingly, ostracize her. The drama in the story has to do principally with how Hester is freed by her acceptance of guilt and, no less importantly, her steadfast refusal to name the father of the child she is carrying, while the townsfolk who shun her are increasingly enslaved by hypocrisy and an unwillingness to be merciful. It's a passion story, in other words—very much like the Gospel According to John, the one that is told almost exclusively from Mary's point of view. But it's Hawthorne's underlying metaphysical assumptions that we are interested in here, and those assumptions first appeared in 1846 when Thoreau climbed Mt. Katahdin in Maine, the event that seeded *Walden*, published in 1854.

Thoreau, as I wrote some ten years ago, is not significant because he conducted an experiment in low-tech living. Rather, he is significant because he was a contemplative on a retreat, and the reason he had become a contemplative was that he quite literally stumbled over the question of questions—why there is something rather than nothing—while scrambling across huge chunks of rock oddly scattered on one of Katahdin's spurs. "Talk of mysteries!" he wrote, in his account of the climb. "Think of our life in nature—daily to be shown matter, to come in contact with it—rocks, trees, wind on our cheeks! The *solid* earth! the *actual* world! . . . *Who* are we? where are we?"[4] It was a transformative moment. After getting back from the Maine woods, Thoreau purchased land adjacent to Walden Pond, built a cabin there, and designed a regimen in which *ora* and *labora* were balanced to the point where he stood a good chance of converting the initially disorienting experience on Mt. Katahdin into consistent and regular orientation toward Being. Result? *Walden*, a book with completely wakeful prose that reads, especially today, like bright water flowing over a gold-pebbled creek bed.

As for Melville, he didn't so much stumble on a rock as merge minds with Shakespeare while reading *King Lear*, the play in which the Bard's profoundly Johannine logic is best on view. That event happened in 1850, during the writing of *Moby Dick*, and it proved as transformative for Melville as the epiphany on Katahdin was for Thoreau. Every single work Melville wrote thereafter shows the same Catholic biases found in *King Lear* and, indeed, the same purpose—that being to "preach truth to the face of falsehood," as Fr. Mapple in the New Bedford whaleman's chapel told Ishmael to do, before the sailor set out with Captain Ahab toward perdition and worse.

Unlike Thoreau, Melville was a superb storyteller who positively glowed when fueled on brandy and cigars. Hence his ability to create alter-egos like Frank Goodman, the sharper in *Confidence Man* (1857) who "slides on humor" into conversation with a completely outclassed fellow operator much as "a pirate schooner with colors flying is landed into the sea on greased ways."[5] Yet he was also a steersman who employed a sextant to "stay on the line" while paying attention to "antlered thoughts," much as "Highland hunters" do when "tracking the snowprints of deer." Those facts, in turn, mean Melville had the skills necessary to be, for us, a modern-day version of Edgar, the character in *King Lear* who skillfully, through playacting, guides the mad and wholly bereft King Lear toward sanity.

My favorite Melville book, these days, is *Israel Potter* (1855), owing chiefly to two "comedic" scenes. In one the hero pretends to be a scarecrow while running from two opposed armies, pointing one way to orient one army and then, moments later, the other way to orient the other army,

4. Thoreau, *Kataadn*, 78–79.

5. Melville, *Confidence Man*, 205.

thereby acting rather like the scarecrow in *The Wizard of Oz*. The other scene? In that one Melville depicts a sea battle between British and American ships as performance by a "joint-stock company" in business to fuel warfare for its own sake, a shocking concept that is relevant in our time, as we find ourselves increasingly subject to strategic "choices"—between, say, "freedom," on one hand, and "democracy," on the other—that are presented as mutually exclusive when, in fact, the alleged choices are really just different versions of a swiftly rising and entirely new form of totalitarianism.

But all Melville's books guide us toward sanity. It really doesn't matter which book of his you reach for. They're all prescient. At the end of *Confidence Man*, as an overhead light enabling a kindly old man to read the Book of Sirach gets turned off, Melville even makes it possible for us to glimpse the true significance of the "committee of safety" now ruling the United States.

And Dickinson? What does she contribute to America's deposit of faith?

The simplest way to answer this question is to note that there is a consistent willingness in Dickinson's posture as a poet to stake all—zero tolerance for pretense; sharply intelligent attention to modest, seemingly insignificant being; and complete readiness to look evil in the eye long enough to *recognize* it and (thereby) defeat it. What could she possibly know about evil, we might innocently ask, given that she lived and died alone, unmarried, in her father's house? Plenty, it turns out, for Dickinson always faces her Maker. She can be playful ("Poor little heart! Did they forget thee? Then dinna care, dinna care!"[6]), bold ("inebriate of air, I am, and debauchee of dew"[7]), and proud ("disdaining men and oxygen"[8]), in addition to being honest ("I con that thing 'forgiven'"[9]) and tough ("temptation's bribe slowly handed back"[10]) but most of her poems are simply records of a deepening relationship with her Maker.

Unlike Melville, Dickinson tended to steer *toward* magnetic north, rather than *by* it, and, as a result, her poems can be harrowing. In one she travels along "great streets of silence" leading to "neighborhoods of pause"[11]; in another she carefully tests the plank Jesus walked before calling it "firm"; and in still another she attributes being quickened by the

6. Johnson, *Complete Poems of Emily Dickinson*, 90.
7. Johnson, *Complete Poems of Emily Dickinson*, 99.
8. Johnson, *Complete Poems of Emily Dickinson*, 135.
9. Johnson, *Complete Poems of Emily Dickinson*, 108.
10. Johnson, *Complete Poems of Emily Dickinson*, 219.
11. Johnson, *Complete Poems of Emily Dickinson*, 517.

Spirit to a master pianist testing key action slowly enough for "your brain to bubble cool" before he "drops full music on" and "deals one imperial thunderbolt that scalps your naked soul."[12]

Back of it all, though, there is gladness and joy, for this woman was consecrated like a Catholic nun is consecrated—"given in marriage" (her words) "unto Thee / Oh Thou Celestial Host, / Bride of the Father and the Son, / Bride of the Holy Ghost."[13] Lucy Beckett, the British author of a fine study of Wallace Stevens's work, even suggests that Gerald Manley Hopkins's only real comparable is Emily Dickinson.[14]

In sum, Hawthorne, Thoreau, Melville, and Dickinson together comprise a homespun but completely reliable foundation for realist biases that are fully in line with the Platonic-Augustinian tradition and *already operative on American soil* given their formative influence on the American mind. Melville called his makeshift theology of being "desperado philosophy," but I think a better name for it would be *perennial philosophy*, pure and simple, the sort that (1) Enlightenment-based philosophers *abandoned* after René Descartes turned the medieval world upside down, (2) phenomenologists (starting with Edmund Husserl) have been trying to *recover*, and (3) ordinary people *use* if ever they should find themselves clinging to the face of a cliff without a rope. Hence, this sort of philosophy can be of considerable worth if ever civilization itself should be on the brink of destruction.

Note, too, that because Hawthorne, Thoreau, Melville, and Dickinson were each wary of organized religion, our American deposit of faith is, to an important extent, *immune* to the ills endangering the Catholic Church and well positioned to serve as interim guardian of the Platonic-Augustinian tradition, should the visible Church collapse and need to be rebuilt. Dickinson was the only one in her class at Mt. Holyoke Female Seminary who refused to stand up when called to identify as "Christian" or "hopeful that she would be." Thoreau was more interested in learning about lotus positions, basmati rice, and the *Bhagavad Gita* than church-going. And Melville openly skewered Church hierarchy with depictions of whalemen looking like "archbisho-Pricks"[15] after they'd donned suits of blubber to protect themselves while boiling whale oil. These anecdotes

12. Johnson, *Complete Poems of Emily Dickinson*, 148.
13. Johnson, *Complete Poems of Emily Dickinson*, 397.
14. Beckett, *In the Light of Christ*, 410–432.
15. Melville, *Moby Dick*, 365.

are funny, in their way, but the really funny part is that publicizing them could play very much in civilization's favor, given that most of the American citizens lining up to vote against laws designed, say, to protect gender "choice" are not, in the normal sense, "religious." Rather, they are truck drivers and waitresses and office workers and even professors who instinctively sense that people who either provide or opt for transgender surgery have taken leave of their senses.

Fault lines have changed!

Except for those among our young who have not yet gotten smartphones and therefore preserved access to wonder, evangelization in the normal sense is over. The question is no longer how to get the Word to people who haven't heard it, or whether you're depressed rather than happy and would do better with Christ in your life. The question now is *what's real*—i.e., what's there whether or not you want it to be there—and whether you will defend this definition in the face of people who want "the real" to be what we, as de-facto gods, wish it to be.

Take the recent foray into Israel by Hamas on the fiftieth anniversary of the Yom Kippur War. That barbaric attack on civilians was a clear instance of evil. Yet most of our college students and a shocking number of our university presidents refuse to acknowledge the attack as such and are cheering the Hamas offensive because Israel is an "occupying power." Are its citizens not entitled to the same respect as citizens from elsewhere? And why is it that "genocide" has become the new rallying cry for those calling on Israel to cease and desist their counter attack? Is it because Israel is guilty of genocide? Or that our university presidents and students are, with their "racism" rallying cry, accusing others of the crime they themselves are advocating for? We need not—indeed, cannot—discuss the deep, elephant-in-the-room reason for these strikes against Israel because that reason can no longer be heard in our now confirmedly post-Christian culture. But we can still talk about reality for at least a few more years, seeing as how the technocracy risen in our midst does not yet control every part of us or every last one of us. And it is our good fortune as Americans to be forced, by the sheer power of the tech companies we've built, to (1) think with Thoreau's and Melville's help about what it might mean for something to be real, (2) weigh the cost of living without it, and (3) in that way earn the right to continue celebrating America as the land of promise it has, so far, proven itself to be.

Shaken Not Stirred

What We Can Learn from James Bond About Western Civ

Amtrak's Pennsylvanian 2024

This year, for me, has been the year of trips, and the one most on my mind is the journey I took to Scotland (source of the back-country ethos that rules Cadiz, Ohio, my adopted hometown), where I spent ten days walking the West Highland Way with my sons—a project that afforded all kinds of adventures, the most "press ready" of which was being mistaken for the actor who played Hellboy in the eponymous 2004 and 2008 film versions of the *Dark Horse* comic-book series. A great honor! But the main adventures were learning terrain, and history keyed by that same terrain.

At Balmaha Harbor, after walking along the shore of Loch Lomond and glimpsing a chain of islands the placement of which indicates (exactly) the whereabouts of the geological fault line dividing Highlands from Lowlands, we learned that *Scot* was the Latin word for *pirate* and referred to folks who settled near the harbor in the fifth and sixth centuries after arriving from Ireland, thereby bringing Gaelic culture to the Scottish Highlands and eventually converting indigenous Picts. At Crienlarich, a crossroads where we left the River Falloch to follow a tributary that drains waters flowing southeast from mountains near Ben Nevis, we passed the ruins of an Augustinian monastery restored by Robert the Bruce in the fourteenth century. All that, before even getting to Kingshouse, an inn where British troops were garrisoned in 1742 after traveling on Cromwellian military roads to put down Jacobites who were trying to restore a Catholic monarch (James II's grandson) to England's throne.

"What *is* Scotland?" my younger son wanted to know early in the trip, after marveling at the medieval "sense" of the town / country interface visible along the West Highland Way, given the absence of suburbia. Me being me, I immediately told him that the way "in" was to read literature, specifically, *Thirty-Nine Steps* author John Buchan's little-known novel *John MacNab* (1925), and Robert Louis Stevenson's *Kidnapped* (1886)—Buchan because of his high-resolution descriptions of trout fishing and cob-booted mountaineering, and Stevenson because of his sympathy for Jacobites and, of course, his de-facto map of the very same Highland route we ourselves were taking.

Kidnapped is set in 1751, just nine years after the Jacobites were defeated at Culloden, and you can learn a lot from Stevenson about their rebellion and the Enclosure Acts that precipitated it. Sure, *Kidnapped* is a boy's adventure tale, but there is something deeper going on. It can, at times, be hard to see through the fog, if you will, of romanticized Gaelic culture that sits thick in *Kidnapped* and, indeed, almost all books by writers who came of age in the late nineteenth century when Catholicism in the Highlands had been eradicated. But, owing to his plot line, Stevenson ultimately enables the reader to grasp that the Jacobites weren't just fighting to restore a Stuart monarch to the throne. In addition, and perhaps even more importantly, they were fighting to reclaim the medieval commons, and life sustained by access to that commons, so as to avoid what they intuited was coming—namely, the demotion of formerly independent Scot farmers into tenant farmers ("crofters") who lived behind a fence and paid rent to a landlord via secondary income derived from employment as a laborer in a quarry (or harvesting kelp on a seashore) until, not too many years later (after owners realized that profit would be better maximized if crofter houses themselves were bulldozed), expelled to America. Which, of course, is what happened between 1750 and 1815 during Highland Clearances, so called.

As the walk with my sons progressed, however, and we found ourselves alongside *Scoti* hikers—all of whom were talking about Britain's upcoming election—I began to doubt whether I had steered my boys in the right direction by recommending they read Buchan and Stevenson. After all, those two writers were, at the very least, comfortable as Unionists, whereas our fellow hikers were most assuredly not. It wasn't just that they were for Scottish independence, which, of course, they were—and to a degree that called to mind the nationalism of William Wallace. Rather, it was that they believed it was "too late" for Scottish independence and were committed to overthrowing Brexit. What was going on?

As you may or may not know, the July 8 election our fellow hikers were talking about turned out to be a landslide victory for the Labour (center left) party in Britain after seventeen years of Conservative (center right) rule, in part because conservatives in Britain were appalled by Prime Minister Rishi Sunak's default on his obligations to trim government spending and show respect for D-Day veterans, and mostly because Britain's problematic separation from the European Union had happened under Conservative rule. In Scotland, though, things turned out to be more complicated, for the dominant party is, and has been for the past seventeen years, the Scottish National Party. And there's the rub. Scotland, unlike England, is not subject to the usual liberal/conservative binary. Instead, it's a place where far-left and far-right folks stand shoulder to shoulder while looking across what appears to be an unbridgeable gulf to more centrist parties on whom they are, confoundedly, dependent.

So my thinking went.

But it wasn't until we drew close to Glencoe, where the River Ba rises and *Skyfall* was filmed, that a lightbulb flicked on in my head and I finally saw the best literary key for deciphering Scotland's uneasy alliance with England.

"Boys," I said. "Forget Buchan and Stevenson. The books you should be reading are Ian Fleming's spy thrillers starring James Bond."

I first got interested in Fleming's novels when a friend claimed that Fleming explicitly referenced Steubenville, Ohio, as *the* training ground, worldwide, for card sharks and dealers with dice-cheat skills in both *Casino Royale*, his first book (1953), and *Diamonds Are Forever*, his fourth (1956). Like a lot of people my age, I had mistakenly imagined that the immensely successful Broccoli/Saltzman movie productions starring Sean Connery contained everything I needed to know about James Bond. Indeed, it had never even occurred to me to read the novels on which the movies are based. Hence when I finally read the novels I was doubly rewarded—first because my friend's claim proved correct, and second because the books were of very high caliber and, in general, far more complex and enjoyable than the movies based on them. If you read the novels straight through, one after the other, it can feel as if you've hitched a ride on the train in *From Russia With Love* (1957) relentlessly boring its way toward a confrontation of importance. By the time you hear the "howl of the windhorn," along with regularly appearing "grade-crossing bells," you're glad to be on that train.

Moreover my interest increased when I discovered that Fleming wrote one Bond book per year, all of them homeruns, over a course of *ten years*—an extraordinary, possibly unparalleled, performance—and that when Fleming did, on his eleventh and final effort, write a bad Bond book (a really bad one, published posthumously in 1965, called *The Man With the Golden Gun*), Robert Ludlum from New York kindly stepped in not only to rescue Fleming and the Bond series from disgrace and oblivion but to *strengthen* that series by writing a more proper sequel to Fleming's tenth book, *You Only Live Twice* (1964). Ludlum called his sequel, published in 1980, *The Bourne Identity*.

Those who have read *You Only Live Twice* will remember the ending, but for those who have not, let's just say that it ends with a literally over-the-top but believable and quite exhilarating sequence in which Bond escapes the villain's castle keep by severing a weather balloon's rope, holding on as helium within the balloon propels the freed device skyward, and then, after being shot by pursuers, falling into the sea, there to be rescued by fishermen. Which is *exactly* where Ludlum in *The Bourne Identity* picks up the plot.

In *You Only Live Twice* the hero is rescued by pearl diver Missy, who swims Bond as a lifeguard might to her fishing village on the other side of a strait.[1] In *The Bourne Identity* the hero is rescued by seamen working on a trawler who drop Bourne off in Marseilles. In each instance it is discovered that the secret agent, upon being shot, has developed amnesia and *does not know who he is*. Indeed, the handoff (if you will) is perfect.

Ludlum was not as good at crafting memorable prose as Fleming was, and at first it seems the ball will be fumbled because Ludlum provides very little in the way of rest spots that ensure a reader's trust. Eventually, though, Ludlum wins you over by carefully detailing how Dr. Marie decides to trust in Bourne's instinctive decision to risk his life to save hers in the face of consistently reliable news that convinces Bourne as well as Marie that he is a trained assassin. The book's best line? "I really know what I'm doing. I think I've always known that."[2] Of course, *The Bourne Identity*

1. Fleming, *You Only Live Twice*, 249–251.
2. Ludlum, *The Bourne Identity*, 519.

became a breakaway success, thereby enabling the production of the Doug Liman-directed movie (and its two sequels) starring Matt Damon, and, on the heels of that success, the rebooting of the entire Bond series via the casting of the sufficiently dangerous and entirely winning Daniel Craig in a thoroughly refreshed version of *Casino Royale*, a competent if not perfect film adaption of Fleming's short story *Quantum of Solace* (1959), and a deliciously perfect, all-stops-removed movie that ratified the Bourne trilogy as a continuation of Bond called—you guessed it—*Skyfall*.

But I digress. My point is that the Bond series is a powerful myth. Indeed, I am convinced that for the past fifty years it has functioned as the twentieth-century edition, as it were, of the Latinized (Virgilian) Homeric myth that has long served, for those of us in the West, as our founding story.

That the Bond series is Homeric is clear for many reasons, foremost among them its reliance on what we would now call comic-book elements, such as villains marked by physical deformities; the regular appearance of exceptionally beautiful, often scantily clad women; and plot devices featuring tricks and disguises that can fail should heretofore fooled observers suddenly recognize a scar. Just as *The Odyssey* features giants (the Cyclops), so too the Bond books feature giants (Mr. Big and the exceptionally tall Dr. No with pincer-like metal hands). As for beautiful women, Vesper (*Casino Royale*), Solitaire (*Live and Let Die*), and Honeychile (*Dr. No*) certainly hold their own with Calypso (the "nymph with lovely braids"), Circe (the enchantress who wears a "filmy" robe drawn close), and Nausicaa (the Phaecian princess who wears nothing at all).

Yet the main reason the Bond series has a Homeric dimension is the figure who makes recognition moments necessary—namely, Bond himself. It's not just that Bond, like Odysseus, is always out in front when it comes time to lead crew members or soldiers into mortal danger (as he does in the underwater sequence in *Thunderball*); rather, it's that he is every bit as deceitful as Odysseus and therefore every bit as prone (when time is ripe) to throw deceit to the wind and, in trademark fashion, announce (for all the world to hear) his real identity: "The name is Bond. James Bond." When that happens in movie versions of the novels, the audience invariably cheers. The reason is that those of us in its midst delight in this recognition moment exactly like we do when Odysseus finally throws caution to the wind after the Cyclops he's just blinded heaves a boulder into the sea perilously close to Odysseus's escaping ship.

"Cyclops!" our hero yells. "If any man on the face of the earth should ask who blinded you, . . . say *Odysseus, raider of cities.* He gouged out your eye. Laertes' son who makes his home in Ithaca."[3]

Note, though, that throughout all these adventures Bond is also Aeneas, a commander who is mannered in his relationships with women and completely, even definitively, devoted to serving the Queen of England and her commonwealth.

The Bond book in which Homeric and Latinized elements are most strongly in view is probably *Dr. No*, due to a prolonged sequence in which Bond actually sails a small wooden craft to Crab Key from Jamaica's northern shore at night under a bowl of stars, much as Odysseus might have done. Moreover, after landing on a beach and crawling under a nearby bush to sleep in safety, Bond wakes to see Honeychile harvesting shells, much as Odysseus wakes to see Nausicaa bathing after he had crawled under an olive bush to sleep in safety after washing up on a beach.[4] But every Bond book written by Fleming features Homeric and Latinized elements. Indeed, the linkage to Homer and Virgil is so strong that, after finishing the series, this reader started to question why people even countenance the idea that James Joyce's *Ulysses* still reigns as the Latinized Homeric epic of our time.

Don't get me wrong. I have great respect for Joyce and *Ulysses* (1922), which takes place over the course of nineteen hours in the quite ordinary lives of Stephen Daedalus (who stands in for Telemachus), Leopold Bloom (who stands in for Odysseus), and Molly Bloom (who stands in for Penelope) as they wander through a morning, an afternoon, and an evening at a hospital, a brothel, a cabman's shelter, a bedroom, a tavern, and a kitchen in Dublin in 1904. It is, without question, a great novel, owing to Joyce's extraordinary skills as a wordsmith and his pioneering stream-of-consciousness narration technique. Additionally, the way he transposes key episodes in the *Odyssey* involving Cyclops and Circe and Odysseus's actual homecoming are ingeniously imagined. But *Ulysses* is an epic solely in an ironic sense, and irony, as a default position, turned out, in the 1960s, to be a dead end. Therefore, it makes sense that, starting in the early part of that decade, as the civilizational ground under our feet began to break along previously undetectable fault lines, the Joycean version of the Latinized Homeric epic might give way to a new version with vast popular appeal

3. Homer, *The Odyssey*, 227.
4. Homer, *The Odyssey*, 167–175.

that became even more vast as it began to be conveyed through movies with soundtracks, as well as through the printed word.

The breakthrough year, clearly, was 1962, for that is when the film version of *Dr. No* was released, starring Sean Connery, Ursula Andress, and—let's face it—John Barry, who wrote the swanky, brass-based score in addition to the trademark surf-guitar riff that accompanies the opening credits of every Bond film. After 1962 the audience for Bond films grew exponentially, and by the time *Thunderball* appeared in 1965 the jury otherwise known as the public had decided that the Bond series was *the* Latinized Homeric epic of our time. Thankfully, the series retained that crown despite bad odds made even worse when producers cast Roger Moore in the starring role starting in 1973.

Looking back, however, you can see that the real miracle was the abiding presence of an underlying, definitely not-planned but highly revealing, structural innovation present in Fleming's edition of our founding story that *highlighted differences* between Homeric and Virgilian visions of how a peace based on the rule of law can be achieved while at the same time *not resolving those differences*: decentralized (federated) polities secured by *Scoti*-like pirates on one hand, and empire projects secured by centurions and navies on the other; the Pleiades and "Orion in all his power" above "broad rich plowland" worked by twelve evenly sized cities on one hand (as depicted on the shield of Achilles[5]), and Roman, British, and American empires extending "far and wide as the earth" on the other (as depicted on the shield of Aeneas[6]). Rather than assuming these viewpoints to be compatible and then simply stirring them together, Fleming's version of the Latinized Homeric epic depended for its efficacy on *shaking up* essentially contradictory aspects to the Homeric and Virgilian viewpoints, much as a bartender might when asked to make an iced martini with vodka and a slice of lemon. The result? An adventure starring James Bond, the ever resourceful, highly dangerous, expertly deceitful *Scoti* pirate from Glencoe whose "secret" Jacobite-like "agent" status enables him to serve Queen and empire while at the same time—thanks to Bond's marriage to Tracy di Vicenzo—maintaining links to organized crime. It's a strange drink, that, but it packs a wallop, and one of the reasons is that it perfectly describes Scotland's strange alliance with Westminster.

5. Homer, *The Iliad*, 483–485.

6. Virgil, *The Aeneid*, 262–265.

Take ex-Prime Minister Sunak's failure to recognize the importance of the memorial marking the eightieth anniversary of D-Day. How could Sunak possibly have decided that a television interview was more important than paying his respects to infantrymen who died so England and its allies might succeed in their effort to vanquish the threat posed by Hitler? At the inn where my boys and I stayed in Tyndrum between Crianlarich and the Bridge of Orchy, our host was appalled by Sunak's absence on a stage where other world leaders had gathered in Normandy. And well our host should have been, given that British, Canadian, and Scottish soldiers, along with First Division American infantrymen leading the D-Day assault at heavily defended Omaha Beach, unquestionably did save Western Europe and, to that extent, the world at large from civilizational collapse in 1944.

Yet it might be more correct to say that these soldiers *forestalled* collapse, owing to the fact that both world wars (themselves phases of a storm generated five hundred years ago when William of Occam removed the Word as an integrative center) occurred while steadily eroding medieval capital still existed and allowed us to maintain the illusion that the West was a Christian culture, even though, as Europe's and now America's rising anti-Catholic sentiment shows, it wasn't.

And, if that hypothesis is correct, might it not also be correct that the ruling power of the technocracy Sunak fronted might have grown to the point where the Roman, British, and American empire projects, along with the Latinized Homeric epic undergirding them, are now obsolete? Surely not. After all, Virgil has oriented us for almost *two millennia*, from the reign of Caesar Augustus up through Dante's and Pope's and Tennyson's and Joyce's times—and even through Fleming's time, when *The Aeneid* oriented and provided purpose for American soldiers maintaining control of straits in the South China Sea, let alone battling their way north through Alpine terrain into Germany from Italy. But, then again, *maybe so* given the accelerating speed with which safety is now displacing liberty as a civilizational principle, and, perhaps even more importantly, the recent sale of Broccoli/Saltzman movie rights to—you guessed it—Amazon.

These are daunting prospects, and cause for worry.

Regarding Civility

Harbor Springs 2024

If you look up the noun "civility" and its adjectival variant "civil" in *Webster's Seventh New Collegiate Dictionary* (published in 1969), you learn up front, in typically brief but very clear form, that "civility" (descending from Middle English, Middle French, and, ultimately, Latin) can mean "politeness" or "courtesy," and that "civil" can mean "civilized," "courteous," or "urbane." And then the editors allow themselves to go to town for a delicious minute or two while differentiating "civil" from its synonyms. "Civil," they state, "suggests no more than a bare minimum fulfillment of the requirements of good breeding and forebearance from roughness or unpleasantness; 'courteous' more actively or dignified politeness; 'gallant' and 'chivalrous' imply courteous attention to women, but 'gallant' suggests dashing behavior and ornate expressions of courtesy, and 'chivalrous' high-minded and self-sacrificing behavior." So many wonderful shades of meaning to choose from! Yet if you search for "training in the humanities" you come up against a brick wall: "*Archaic*."

Game over!

That sounds like a joke, and, of course, in one sense it is, but in another sense it isn't, for we in the West have for the last five hundred years been living on borrowed time ever since monastic orders in the early fourteenth century started to grant legal permission to peasants farming an agricultural commons (rather than tacitly respecting customary rights) at the exact same time that exceptionally bright minds within those same monastic orders made still other changes that effectively removed incarnational logic as our organizing cultural principle. William of Occam, for example, began to think of the conceptual aspect to words as a hindrance to understanding, rather than an aid, before then going on to up the ante still further by *opposing* freedom to obedience and defining freedom as a "power" that allows a person to "indifferently and contingently produce an effect." After moves like that, paths were open for thinkers like René Descartes to come along and upend medieval sciences in favor of modern ones with vastly greater predictive power.

Rather than growing capital built up in the Middle Ages, we have (for all kinds of reasons, many of them good) been drawing it down, and ever since the first election of Trump it has become increasingly clear that the well enabling drawdowns has gone dry, as online dictionaries succeeding *Webster's New Collegiate Dictionary*, along with the appearance of new projects dedicated to reducing polarization both make clear. According to *vocabulary.com*, "civil" now means "speaking kindly to someone who has hurt your feelings," and according to *The Institute for Civility*, "civility" now means "claiming and caring for one's identity needs and beliefs without degrading someone else in the process." Meanings that involve self-sacrifice? Those are no longer in view.

Moreover, this change in meaning has happened with astonishing speed. Just two years ago I was asked to give a talk at the annual *New Polity* conference about whether America is a tyrannical state, and, I must confess, upon learning the topic I thought conference organizers were crazy. America a tyranny? I couldn't even compute that. Had the conference organizers been reading too much Del Noce or Manent or even (bless her) Arendt? After all, this is America we were talking about—the land tall ships sailed to from every corner of the globe in 1976, the land of Melville and Thoreau, the land of Robert Stone and Richard Ford and Cormac McCarthy, even—upping this list now to a slightly higher notch—the land of Pea Eye and Deets and *Hat Creek Cattle Company* owner Woodrow F. Call and his determinedly literate, constantly antagonistic friend and co-owner Augustus McCrae! How could one even countenance the *idea* of America as a tyranny when writers like Larry McMurtry were walking across its plains and through its streets free as birds? Calling our country a tyranny was as manifestly absurd as calling it systemically racist. Negative liberties matter, they are still operative, and lest there was doubt on either of these scores conference attendees had only to remember or imagine walking out of a brick-and-mortar prison featuring guard towers and steel gates and guards into the hustle and bustle of an urban city where, despite horns and the clear and present danger of getting mugged, policemen by and large stood guard to protect our liberties.

Yes, there were indications that American governmental powers could in the future become tyrannical, given the increasing prevalence of "cancel culture" as a means of ensuring "safe" democratic speech "environments," and the increasing stridency of claims regarding gender that rivaled, for sheer falseness, the sort of claims that used to be made, fifty years ago, by the agitprop department of the Soviet Communist Party's famed Central Committee. But these challenges didn't, at the time, seem insurmountable. Proposed "post-liberal" solutions seemed foolish rather than scary; currently inadequate conservative solutions dating from the Reagan and Bush eras could be improved to the point where they more successfully met looming challenges; and, as for agitprop departments in our administrative state, we could still laugh at the punchline in Paul McCartney's wonderful song, "Back in the USSR."

But now?

Let's just say that a lot of us aren't laughing any more.

Many if not most conservatives in this country imagine that the English common law tradition and indeed the English language itself (think Churchill, let alone Middle English) can somehow immunize the American people against absolutism descending from Czarist Russia, the Austro-Hungarian empire, and, most importantly, the ancien régime in France. But it can't. Contra Burke and his descendant Russell Kirk, the English and French revolutions were not opposites in the real sense. Instead, they were two different aspects of the same societal disruption that Dutch historian Johan Huizinga documented in *The Waning of the Middle Ages*. Locke's contractual language as on view in his *Second Treatise on Government* (1698) was a model for Rousseau when the famous lover-botanist put forward, in 1762, the idea of a "social" contract. Moreover Rousseau wrote in reaction to coercive force exhibited by oligarchs in Calvinist Geneva just as Locke had written in reaction to coercive force employed by Jacobite kings, and Rousseau also set his deliberations in a "state of nature" that was very like Hobbesian-Lockean states of nature because its fields and woods featured individuals unformed (as if that could be possible) by tradition.

Hence the currently reigning National Conservative "populist" brain trust to an important degree refreshed the standard Left v. Right standoff by harnessing Catholic energies to critique classical liberalism rather than communism and enable neocons, so called, to see the devastating impact of free trade agreements and the importance of not outsourcing manufacturing industries like steelmaking.

By the same token, however, it would be a mistake to assume that post-liberal conservatism is any less related (or less opposed) to essentially communist progressive energy than Reagan-era conservativism was. The truth is that all major brands of conservatism in this country (be it in *National Review* circa 1954, *First Things* circa 1994, or *Compact* circa 2024) comprise one of two different aspects of what's left over after the removal of Western civilization's integrative center, and the problem is that when we commit to one or the other of these two aspects (depending on how we view Trump's occasional lack of civility), we create a reversing current (driven by conservatives on one side and progressives on the other) that grows a technocracy which is actualizing the largest enclosure act in the history of the West.

Consider the Great Reset project officially launched by Klaus Schwab in June 2020 to capitalize (pun intended) on opportunities presented by a COVID-19 event that had earlier been carefully simulated two different times by the same people who stood to gain from the reset. The altruistic goal there was "stakeholder" capitalism, which is something quite different from "shareholder" capitalism. Instead of arranging for, say, small middle-class businesses to succeed, the Great Reset wiped them out in order more efficiently to advance agenda items comprising an allegedly more real common good consisting of carbon-free energy, sustainable agriculture, historical preservation, and, best of all, "solidarity." Result? A concentration of smoothly functioning top-down coercive power that even Thomas Hobbes would be awed by, given that this same reset will accelerate the conversion of cash-based economies into digital ones so that every transaction can be tracked and stored in data clouds that, with World Bank assistance, generate money (for those operating the levers) like real clouds generate rain.

What's even more remarkable, though, is that almost all of the corporations serving as Klaus's biggest partners and sponsors, be they merchandise providers like Amazon or asset managers like BlackRock, are American. Moreover, the combined market capitalization of Alphabet, Amazon, Apple, Metaverse and Microsoft now outranks the gross GDP of Germany, France, and Italy combined.

Note too that it is not "they" who are doing this. On the contrary, we are. We live, most of us, in a society where our every wish is not only catered to but even granted by an entire team of well-funded Metaverse employees who have not only foreseen our every wish but also arranged for auctions to occur so whole companies can compete to be noticed by us, the new royal "we," and thereby all the better serve our needs. And then consider, next, that this same technocracy ensures perpetual, which is to say immortal, self-oriented life by permanently entrapping us in false opposites, thereby sealing doors that in older, less advanced times provided occasions for getting outside and, well, seeing the stars. Remember truth? That which was there whether or not we wanted it to be there? Thanks to our new technocratic state this transcendental is now a thing of the past. Instead of conventional definitions of truth, we have "my-truth-your-truth," and, frankly, life works out better that way because equality is a less cumbersome first principle. The best principle is to respect every opinion, no matter how demented, in part because all people are equal and every person matters, but mostly because we kinda like Huey Long's idea that every man should be a king.

Which means: our future is bright.

In April of 2024 I drove up to a small town east of Cleveland to stand in the "path of totality," which was awarded by fate to Plattsburg, NY, Erie, PA, Little Rock, AR, and Dallas, TX in the form of an eclipse of the sun. Normally I would have watched the event on a piece of paper. Who needs totality? It was easier and just as informative to watch the event by using a cardboard pinhole projector while standing on my own deck. But then I asked myself a question: what are the chances that our moon is exactly the right size and distance from Earth to block out the sun so exactly that there is a ring-of-stars effect as sunlight travels through canyons on the moon to reach us? One in five zillion? True, in another fifty million years, the moon will have moved far enough away that all eclipses will be annular, but for us, now, the moon blocks the sun *perfectly*. So I decided to go. And found myself walking onto a football field where lower middle-class Americans of every political persuasion, every conceivable color, and consistently impeccable attention to fashion had a party going on with lawnchairs and boom boxes and blankets and frisbees in mid-flight and tacos imported from food trucks and an emcee with a microphone at the fifty yard line interviewing astrophysicist experts as a big digital stopwatch on the scoreboard ticked its way toward "totality." *Goodness gracious, great balls of fire*. What in heck were we doing here, I wondered. Until, after carefully donning cardboard-mounted eyeware, we all looked up, grew quiet, and wept during the four-minute interval in which time widened, the world grew still, and evening and morning airs stirred nearby leaves and grasses.

Never mind that April 8th was the Feast of the Asumption in the 2024 liturgical calendar and that we were, to that very extent, invited to see what Aztecs saw in 1531 when they glimpsed, in fact and through Aztec prophecy, a pregnant woman who so exactly displaced their sun god, Huitzilopochtli, that they (some nine million of them) effortlessly and almost instantly became Christians—which is to say, carriers of Western Civ. The important thing, here, is that those of us who were on that football field knew, during four very long minutes, that we were fellow citizens and, to that extent, carriers of whatever civilization might be dawning. Did we also know that the West, as presaged by our perfection of instantaneous communication and the concurrent obsolescence of "civility" defined as "training in the humanities," is ending? Probably not. All that can be said for sure is that America turns out to be the place where our founding story ends and something new—call it a new "heaven" and a new "earth"—comes into view. Assuming, of course, that we do our job, accept the role history has assigned to us, and keep watch as sentinels posted on a hilltop keep watch.

Why Cormac McCarthy Stands Alone Among Novelists

Hanover Ridge 2024

I came late to McCarthy, probably because, having fallen under the spell of Robert Stone in my early twenties after reading *Dog Soldiers* (Stone's 1971 novel about a war correspondent in Vietnam running afoul of a drug cartel after trying to smuggle Asian heroin into Oakland, California), I was predisposed to doubt and then, after reading follow-up prose in *A Flag for Sunrise* (1981) and *Children of Light* (1986), flat-out dismiss claims that any current-day writer could be as good as Stone. Moreover, when publishers aggressively promoted Stone's fifth novel, *Outerbridge Reach* (1992) by comparing him to Melville, I assented, at which point I quit reading novels altogether for about ten years while doing historical research for a book about eastern Ohio and the trans-Allegheny West.

Upon completing that writing project, though, I started to read novels again—chiefly as a means for blowing off steam, but also because I had begun to wonder whether the American mind, so called, could continue to support the production of great novels, given what I'd learned over the course of writing my book—and came across McCarthy's "Border Trilogy." Which I marveled at. These tales starring John Grady in Mexico and, in particular, Billy Parham under a freeway overpass somewhere west of Albuquerque didn't just nail the west Texas cowboy myth; they actually elevated that myth to a level customarily reserved for three thousand-year-old myths commemorating Greek gods. And then along came McCarthy's post-apocalyptic father-son novel *The Road*, a tale of light shining in darkness. Where had I been all these years, while bemoaning the loss of word-based knowledge as a default cultural position? What with Richard Ford and, now, Cormac McCarthy in addition to Robert Stone, we were going to be fine, for America had produced not just one but three superbly talented novelists who could stand with Saul Bellow, John Updike, and Philip Roth. But then McCarthy died, and suddenly I was looking at a whole new set of what seemed to be preposterously adulatory claims occasioned by the posthumous publication (in 2023) of two long-awaited novels about physics, the atom bomb, and the existence of God called *The Passenger* and *Stella Maris*. So, I read those two books. And was ri-vet-ed.

The Passenger opens with its main character, Bobby Western, wrapped in an emergency blanket and sipping hot tea at 3:00 AM in an inflatable raft anchored near a submerged plane a couple miles south of New Orleans. There's a Coast Guard cutter at anchor one hundred yards to the west, and in the seat next to him there's a tender in radio conversation with a diver twenty feet down who is cutting his way into the plane's fuselage with an acetylene torch. To the north, lights on trucks headed east on Interstate 90 toward Pass Christian move "like beads of moisture on a string," and the air smells of oil mixed with "the rich tidal funk of mangrove and salt grass from the islands."[1] How deep can you use acetylene? the tender asks. Thirty, thirty-five feet, Bobby explains. And after that it's oxyarc? Yes. At that Bobby pulls on his weight belt, fits a regulator to his mouth, and steps off the raft to join the welder who has just swum into the plane. It's a small private jet. Co-pilot and passengers seem to have died calmly in their seats, and in the cockpit the avionic board with vertical speed indicators has been ripped out of the instrument panel. The flight bag? Missing.

Welding tradecraft, steadily rising suspense, attention to the natural world, hints of deep water on metaphysical as well as literal levels—all that is established in a mere thirty pages. And that's before even meeting the cast of characters who expertly "do" Borscht Belt comedy and Shakespearean monologues when it comes time to convey the book's chief themes.

I got a little worried when, two-thirds of the way through *The Passenger*, McCarthy appears to turn from the mystery of the submerged jet and a related, highly suspenseful episode on an offshore oil rig during a hurricane to focus instead on an extended trip from Texas to Montana during which, penniless, Western survives hunger and extreme cold by trapping small animals, sleeping in abandoned farmhouses, and protecting coals

1. McCarthy, *The Passenger*, 19–27.

from each and every cookfire. Upon going back, though, to an italicized introductory chapter told from the point of view of Western's sister, Alice, I realized that Western's journey north was not a detour. Rather, it was bringing to fruition a carefully planted seed that, upon ripening, could function as the end toward which all action in *The Passenger* was pointing. In short, McCarthy appeared to know what he was doing. And when I read *Stella Maris*, the transcript of taped conversations between Alice and a psychiatrist employed by a clinic she'd committed herself to, I had proof that McCarthy knew what he was doing.

All told, these last two crucially linked novels by McCarthy comprise a stunning achievement. Sustained attention to how manual laborers work, the history of Oppenheimer's Manhattan project, views of bollarded Libyan freighters along the shore of the Mississippi River beneath New Orleans, partitas by Bach, what it's like to drive a race car, and, particularly, a field of mathematics called topo theory through which reality itself becomes a subject—these seemingly incommensurable jigsaw-puzzle pieces wind up fitting together perfectly, owing to an overarching story about what it means to carry another's pain.

Okay, I thought. McCarthy really might have been America's best novelist during the second half of the twentieth century, and if that's the case, I ought to revise my yardstick for determining greatness.

Then something funny happened on the way to the forum where American matters of importance are settled. Upon studying reviews of McCarthy's work, I discovered that the avalanche of praise attending the posthumous publication of his final two books wasn't really generated by those last two books at all. Rather, it was generated by *Blood Meridian*, a book McCarthy had written almost forty years earlier, just prior to his Border Trilogy project.

According to critics, *Blood Meridian* was McCarthy's masterpiece.

I was skeptical, and even a little annoyed, given that the book turned out, once again, to be about men on horseback, albeit the bad kind—scalphunters—as opposed to cowboys proper with codes of honor. Yet, determined as I was to see this adventure through, I fast-tracked *Blood Meridian* to the top of my to-read pile and quickly discovered that, despite spectacular payoffs owing to a clear debt to Herman Melville, the book did not deserve the praise it got, owing (partially) to an equally clear debt to William Faulkner, whose grandiose sentences with seven, eleven—heck, sometimes even thirteen—clauses are often lengthy simply to disguise the fact that, at bottom, the "thought" being expressed is incoherent and doesn't say anything. In the main, though, McCarthy's problem in *Blood Meridian* isn't his penchant for long sentences with almost zero punctuation. Rather, it's that his attention to cobbled prose and landscape often gets in the way of plot and character development. Indeed, many of the characters in *Blood Meridian* (the "Kid" excepted) arrive fully drawn and then depart unchanged, and here I think especially of Judge Holden, the Ahab-like figure who assembles the team of bounty-hunter "renegades" so as to "federate" them along "one keel" to the point where, with the desert floor beneath their horses' hooves "humming like a snare drum," the company can effectively mock a world made by a Creator who didn't ask the judge's permission before bringing it into being.

It took me a while to figure out exactly why reviewers were stretching when assessing *Blood Meridian*, but eventually—like a guy getting a joke one day late—this blockhead "got it." Reviewers were stretching not because they were hucksters or had sensed an opportunity to jump on a bandwagon actually going somewhere, but because they had correctly intuited greatness without having access to the right hermeneutic. What is the right hermeneutic? It's that McCarthy, a little before the rest of us, had caught a glimpse of Western Civilization's end. Hence, his interest in how things *look* in this novel, rather than narrative suspense: ruined churches and violated sanctuaries, Orion rising in the east "like an electric kite," aspen leaves lying on black dirt in the trail like "golden disclets,"[2] and (upon arrival at the Pacific) "tidepools bright as smelter pots" near a horse on the beach looking west "past men's knowing" toward whales that "ferry their vast souls through the black and seamless sea."[3] *Blood Meridian*, it turns out, was primarily a painting rather than a novel proper, but owing to McCarthy's skills as a novelist, this was hard to see.

Was it right for reviewers to single out *Blood Meridian* as crucially important?

In order to answer this question, we need to look again at the writer mentioned at the beginning of this reflection, namely, Robert Stone.

McCarthy and Stone have a lot in common. They were born in eastern cities within four years of each other (McCarthy in Providence, Rhode Island, in 1933, Stone in Brooklyn, New York, in 1937), they attended Catholic

2. McCarthy, *Blood Meridian*, 142–144.

3. McCarthy, *Blood Meridian*, 316.

parochial schools, they went straight into the military after graduating from high school (McCarthy to the Air Force, Stone to the Navy), and they wrote their first books in New Orleans (McCarthy arrived in 1962, Stone in 1960) before then emigrating west—in McCarthy's case to Texas by way of Ibiza, Spain, and in Stone's case to California by way of Vietnam. Note, too, that their first books (*Outer Dark*, in McCarthy's case, *Hall of Mirrors* in Stone's) feature main characters who hail from east Tennessee hill country, just as later books (*The Passenger* in McCarthy's case and *Flag for Sunrise* in Stone's) feature crucial visionary moments cued by divers getting a sense of the depths beneath them as they work close to, or over, the Cayman Trench in the Caribbean Sea. And, lastly, note that in all their books McCarthy and Stone are as comfortable "speaking" Catholic tropes as they are gifted at discerning cultural trends destined to key the age we live in now.

Here (in this latter sense) I think especially of how they spot the arrival of conspiracy thinking as a default position through extended talk about the assassination of JFK in McCarthy's *The Passenger*, on the one hand, and a sustained depiction of a MAGA-type rally circa 1962 in Stone's *Hall of Mirrors*, on the other. (Stone's glimpse of Trump's coming appeal is surreal in its accuracy and brimming with insight.[4] Think patriots, eagles with lightning bolts in their talons, states' rights, and free enterprise vs. atheistic communism—all set to the 1960 instrumental surf-riff hit "Walk Don't Run," by The Ventures.)

Yet, despite this dizzyingly extensive list of what McCarthy and Stone have in common, these two writers inhabit radically different worlds.

You might think this is because Stone (who spent his entire career teaching, either at an Ivy League school or at a prestigious writing workshop) is a progressive—that is to say, a person who believes that people who try to separate reason from faith are in an important sense enlightened and (to that narrow extent) licensed to act in a patronizing manner toward benighted people who, naturally, require wake-up calls regarding an allegedly natural disposition toward bigotry—whereas McCarthy (who never even once taught at an institution) isn't. But that conclusion would be wrong, for Stone is familiar with hatred and consistently trains razor-sharp, ultra-logical eyes on how we all make rational decisions to behave in self-destructive ways. No, the real reason Stone and McCarthy inhabit different worlds is that the Judeo-Christian civilization otherwise known

4. Stone, *Hall of Mirrors*, 103–117.

as "the West" is for Stone in full swing as a force to be reckoned with and battled against, whereas for McCarthy it is already past.

What, then, did McCarthy see after catching a glimpse of the evening aspect to the West? What did he see that Stone couldn't see, given that he (McCarthy) was standing in a world quite different from the "new" one unwittingly established by Columbus that Stone still resided in?

Quite simply and completely without irony or apology, it is the enduring presence of Christ—or, more exactly, Jesus and Mary, star of the sea—and the reliability of the promise implicit in the Incarnation, the Passion, and Mary's Assumption.

You can see this bias taking shape in *No Country For Old Men*, but it wasn't until McCarthy conceived *The Road*, a book where the plot's pretext is seemingly complete darkness ensuing after a nuclear holocaust, that the wave this bias comprises was able to break with full force on the shores of McCarthy's imagination. In 2012, when I first read *The Road*, that pretext seemed like a clever dystopian device, but now when you read the novel you see that McCarthy was playing for keeps, because the book turns out not only to be about the importance of "carrying fire"[5] in a world where gray snowflakes expire like "the last host of Christendom"[6] and the ocean itself "heaves like a vat of slag."[7] In addition, *The Road* is laced with realist emphases relating to the importance of names and what it might mean to lose them as well as the things they signify.

And then along comes *The Passenger* and *Stella Maris*.

The tuning fork for both these novels is a scene in the preface to *The Passenger* where a hunter in Wisconsin comes across a dead woman in woods filling with snow. The hunter doesn't know how to pray but he knows he must, so he stogs his gun in the snow and gets down on his knees. "Tower of ivory," he says. "House of gold." He kneels for a long time, and then, upon rising, he sees a splash of red owing to a bright scarf that he hadn't noted when he first found the woman, at which point McCarthy adds, "Some bit of color in the scrupulous desolation. On this . . . cold and barely spoken Christmas day."[8] *Barely spoken!* After that stunner, there is no let-up: Alice dreaming about the importance of "keeping the train in view" rather than just following the tracks; Bobby Western looking from the

5. McCarthy, *The Road*, 276–278.
6. McCarthy, *The Road*, 16.
7. McCarthy, *The Road*, 215.
8. McCarthy, *The Passenger*, 3.

inflatable raft toward trucks driving east toward Pass Christian; chapters further in where the reader is reminded again and again of Mary's status as tabernacle and her christening as the new Eve; chapters near the end where there is sustained philosophical attention to reality concluding with "if you sound everything to its source you have to come to an intention"; and, at the end of *Stella Maris*, "I will be their eucharist."[9]

The bottom line here is that, despite McCarthy's self-generated "last pagan on earth" ID tag, he is the best, most reliably Catholic literary artist this country has produced since Flannery O'Connor.

9. McCarthy, *Stella Maris*, 190.

III

Fear and Trembling in Las Vegas

North Las Vegas 2024

When I first read Kierkegaard's *Either/Or,* the book which (along with Shakespeare's *King Lear* and Dante's *Commedia*) led me from a decidedly unchurched upbringing into the Catholic Church and then (following Abraham) to Ohioan hill country, it never occured to me that, as an American, I might one day discover myself to be dependent on regular sightings of Vegas to navigate and think clearly.

I mean—seriously. Vegas? The town built in 1931 on desert wasteland to house and service engineers, explosive experts, cement truck operators and Apache highwall climbers building Hoover Dam and then (starting in the late thirties) mobsters who needed a place to launder their money? Impossible. Sure, Elvis Presley had a second life thanks to Vegas residency before dying at Graceland in 1977; therefore, the city figures prominently in nearly every American's mind thanks to the king's inestimable importance as the man who best personified the reversing current that still powers our trans-Allegheny West. Also it is true that I am personally familiar with Nevada's basin-and-range topography thanks to my journey east. But—mentally grounded by Vegas? That seemed unlikely. Yet, upon opening my eyes, I have to concede it's true. As Kierkegaard would say in a salute to Abraham, "Here am I."

Hineni!

How, then, did this happen? What have I done? Am I here simply because, once in a lifetime, water flows underground?

The real answer is twofold and a lot more prosaic than the Talking Heads version. First, my wife and I found ourselves on a Vegas runway one year ago last Christmas after boarding a connecting flight to Vancouver, WA, so as to meet a new grandson, and, with night coming on, our jet taxied past a large spherical building I'd never seen before or even imagined. What was *that*, I asked myself, and then, as if on cue, our pilot banked the plane hard to the west so we could see that the building appeared to be a giant wide-awake eyeball looking up toward the heavens, in addition to being spherical. Needless to say I did some homework upon arriving in Vancouver and discovered that the just-completed building, owned by Madison Square Garden, featured exterior and interior skins that functioned as intensively pixelated LED screens that can be programmed to change upon demand. Two days before I first saw the structure, it was a beach ball. A week later it was the planet otherwise known as Earth—gorgeous in its blueness—as it appears upon being viewed from space.

So that is one reason.

The other is that, to my wife's consternation and mine also, her nephew scheduled a July wedding in Vegas. What was he thinking? we wondered. It's hot in Vegas during the summertime, it's a long way from the verdant hills he was born in, and a wedding in Vegas is sure to be tacky. But of course we had to go. So, on the hottest day ever recorded in Vegas for July, we arrived and found ourselves standing as witnesses in a leafy bird sanctuary for an exchange of vows spoken within a traditional Judeo-Christian format; dealing with a stunningly competent, fireman-based first-responder team who arrived (quickly) to treat my brother-in-law for heat stroke; going to Sunday mass downtown at the original (thriving) "cottage parish" for Vegas established in 1908 just north of what is now the Strip; visiting a veterans cemetery whose only real comparable is Arlington Cemetery in Virginia; and marveling at the unexpected splendor of the current-day Strip after taking a wrong turn and finally seeing (viscerally as well as intellectually) how different current-day Vegas is from the Vegas I thought I knew from the research I'd done while writing an essay about Steubenville's role in the creation of casinos (like Desert Inn where Sinatra debuted, and The Sands where the Rat Pack performed).

Vegas, it turned out, had not just one but *three* eras geared to time-specific lures fronted by musical, theatrical, and sporting events, which together comprised and in some important sense defined America.

There was "early" Vegas, galvanized by the construction of the Pair-o-Dice Club in 1931 just south of town at the top of what eventually became (in 1938) the Strip, featuring Wilbur Clark's (Cleveland-controlled) Desert Inn one mile south on (yes) Par-a-dise Road, built in 1950, and Meyer Lansky's (Havana-controlled) Sands, built a couple years later just south of Desert Inn's golf course. The lure for each of these places, needless to say, was legally instituted gambling fronted by showgirls, singers like Dean Martin, and PGA tournaments staged on Desert Inn fairways. Then, in 1966, Howard Hughes and Kirk Kerkorian bought up most of the early Vegas properties, thereby ushering in a new "transitional" era defined by heavy-weight boxing tournaments featuring the likes of Leon Spinks, residency musical acts like Tom Jones at Caesar's Palace in 1969, an incredible 636 straight sold-out Westgate (Las Vegas Hilton) shows by mob-beholden Elvis Presley from 1969 to 1976, and, last but not least, the publication of gonzo journalist Hunter S. Thompson's hugely successful *Fear and Loathing in Las Vegas* in 1971, and, one year later, Denise Scott Brown's and Robert Venturi's immensely influential *Learning From Las Vegas*, the Yale School of Art and Architecture research project summation which found in Strip signage a means for questioning whether form should ever follow function, as modernist architects had long assumed.

This latter "transitional" period lasted about as long as the first one did, all the way to 1997, at which point the New York–New York resort opened and a "new" Vegas appeared, whose lures (presaged as much by Elvis' white-suited imitation of himself as by Vegas' placement on land very like the Sahara desert) were simulations of Egyptian obelisks, the Eiffel Tower, and Venetian canals, let alone the Chrysler Building, the Statue of Liberty, and Brooklyn Bridge. These resorts were each of them fronted (sustained) by residency acts like Blue Man Group, Andre Agassi's showy climb to the pinnacle of professional tennis, and, most recently, U2.

That's an astonishing array of acts, and, curiously, all of them age well except Hunter Thompson's *Fear and Loathing in Las Vegas*.

That book, told as it is in full-tilt confessional mode, is an "expanded" version of an article Thompson wrote for *Sports Illustrated* about the Mint 500 off-road racing event on sand hills between Las Vegas and the Nevada-California state line, and the first thirty pages of the book have a lot of promise, given that Thompson's drug-induced states are not a lot different from the "straight" takes on Haight-Ashbury and the Vietnam war that were being televised on nightly news shows at the time he was writing.

Moreover, as the book's subtitle (*A Savage Journey to the Heart of the American Dream*) indicates, Thompson's all-in bet on Vegas' looming importance could have yielded spectacular returns. Soon, though, Thompson loses control, owing to his selection of Horatio Algier as a tuning fork, his unfailingly smug contempt for unenlightened cops from Michigan and Ohio backcountry, and his explicitly stated, astonishingly trite conclusion that Catholic doctrinal claims amount to a hat trick weighing approximately as much as Timothy Leary's claims regarding cosmic harmony do. In short, Thompson fails in his attempt to deliver on his opening-page promise that, if we hold on long enough, the ride he offers will be worth the risk. He did get close. You can't help but laugh when an informant finally locates the American Dream out "on Paradise Road, somewhere in the Las Vegas area," before adding that the dream "burned down three years ago."[1] But that laugh isn't worth as much as the cigar he promised we'd be smoking.

How then (after getting Vegas's three periods clearly in view) can it be argued that Las Vegas grounds us as Americans?

It's not just that this city serves as a touchstone for those of us who are still engaged in culture wars, as became clear when *The New Yorker* ran an article on the fiftieth anniversary of Brown's and Venturi's *Learning From Las Vegas*, in which it was argued that their "deadpan" take on Strip architecture enabled revolution in the sixties sense and still enables it today. Or that this city has steadily rising financial clout, thanks to the success of Allegiant Air (ostensibly founded in 1997 to serve small midwestern cities but in fact founded to ensure allegiance to "new" Vegas); the completion of two-billion dollar Allegiant Stadium (ostensibly built to host the Las Vegas née Oakland Raiders but in fact built to host the 2024 Super Bowl) and the anticipated construction of a new ball park on the ruins of the Tropicana for pro-baseball's (no longer Oakland-based) Athletics. Or even that the only real comparable to Vegas is Dallas, a city which occupies a similarly foundational if traumatic place in our national psyche, owing to its link to the JFK assassination and, to that degree, organized crime while at the same time manifesting continued financial (think oil/gas) and cultural (think Dallas Museum of Art) importance.

Rather, it's that Vegas is taking simulation—as a project—to a whole new level.

1. Thompson, *Fear and Loathing*, 168.

Let's look again at the MSG Sphere which so surprised me when the pilot of the jet my wife and I were riding on granted himself a good look at the structure.

From the runway and even from the air the Sphere looked relatively small compared to the Stratosphere Tower, Steve Wynn's Encore building, and, well, the Trump Tower on West Desert Inn Road. But the modesty of the new building's size is deceptive, for this Sphere is a game-changer. Though architects in Vegas now claim that "theming" is on its way out, it would probably be more accurate to say that one *kind* of theming is giving way to a different one in which the goal is to simulate Creation rather than just civilizations. Remember Arthur C. Clark's first novel, *The City and the Stars* (published in 1956) about Diaspar, the last and (owing to its sealed aspect) final city on planet Earth? That, I submit, is what is slowly but surely being built in Vegas every time its hospitality-design experts get called on to build "the next great integrated resort" for clients in Singapore, Macau, South Africa, and Dubai. These Vegas architects are thinking, every day, about "integrated interior space" featuring the same easy pedestrian access to ponds, markets, and craft-specific shops that medieval towns once featured in resorts large enough to fill thousands of hotel rooms at once, and, to that very extent, they are unwittingly building the rudiments of what will eventually become Diaspar. Is this hunch far-fetched? Maybe so. Then again, maybe not, for popular culture still reigns as our best adjudicator of important trends, and *BladeRunner 2049* was, strikingly, set in Las Vegas rather than Los Angeles.

Note too that successfully simulating Creation under one roof requires that everything under that same roof, be it guests or wiring, is legible (i.e., "readable") to computers, and, that being the case, it is only a matter of time before reading in the prayerful sense becomes obsolete, thereby guaranteeing that we will lose our minds let alone the means to question the legitimacy or rightness of what is coming.

Indeed, there are signs that we've already lost that means.

In early 2016, after the Democratic party had been blindsided by the election of Donald Trump, there was fierce resistance from virtually every left-leaning person or institution as ordinary people, members of Congress, and, basically, the entire staff of *The New York Times* plotted to remove him from office by almost any means. This year, 2024, when Mr. Trump's victory was less of a surprise and harder to contest owing to the decisiveness of election results, people on the left have started to resort instead to concepts of a "multiverse" featuring an infinite number of "timelines," some of which deserve more allegiance than others, owing to varying degrees of promise, much as atheists proposed the existence of parallel universes as a way to maintain their belief that life evolved by chance despite mounting evidence that it couldn't. Moreover, it is not just left-leaning individuals having recourse to this idea. David Friedberg, co-host of the "All In" tech podcast, employed the timeline concept to convey elation at Mr. Trump's recent victory by citing *The Matrix*, which, of course, was about living inside a manufactured, actively controlled dream. "We're on this timeline," he said, "and I do think the United States, as Neo, dodged a lot of bullets here."[2]

Given, then, that we are now choosing which "reality" to inhabit, has not a serious corner been turned?

I believe it has. I believe we have to some extent entered the city so frighteningly described in the opening pages of Arthur C. Clark's science fiction classic, *The City and the Stars*, where the antagonist, Alvin, chooses which simulated "world" he'd next like to enter.

It's only been two years since Henry Kissinger was ridiculed by Noam Chomsky for being alarmed at the appearance of ChatGPT, but already Kissinger's warning seems out-of-date, given the degree to which he underestimated the threat. It's not just that Sam Altman's Open AI, China's Deepthink, and Musk's xAI pose grave dangers because, turbo-charged as they soon will be by data centers enwrapping the entire globe with their endless library-like stacks of cooling trays full to the brim with graphic processing units, AI bots will be able to perfect drone warfare, worsen social inequality, and systematically generate "deep fakes," as G7 leaders and the late Pope Francis of blessed memory have all recently pointed out. Or even that, thanks to widespread automation, massive job loss, and the institution of a government-supplied universal basic income, AI may destroy any and all chances of getting rich. Rather, it's that previously unavoidable "chores" like reading and writing, which involve listening to prompts from a world not designed by us, are being intentionally jettisoned. That's the biggest danger, and once you grasp this new danger you quickly realize that the choice we face is not whether to install regulatory frameworks so that, as a society, we can safely "maximize" AI benefits. That would be a ridiculous goal, every bit as ridiculous as the now rather quaint goal of policing smartphone use during class. And that fact, in turn, suggests that our ultimate choice is no longer deference to oracular AI utterances v. reasonable faith, as Kissinger

2. Zoffer, "Try a Different Timeline."

thought, or strong towns v. big tech as localists still think. Rather, it may be, as Arthur C. Clark so memorably conveys, inside v. outside, with "inside" premised on consenting to simulated intelligence, and "outside"[3] premised on committing to the act St. Thomas Aquinas referred to as *intelligere*, "the proper operation of the human being as such."

I say "we," but, as intimated earlier, many of us have already decided to live in Diaspar full-time, and as that number grows it will become harder to resist the swelling tide. Thankfully, a fair number of us have *anchors* out that permit us to remain unmoved by the tide, and here I think especially of (1) casino owners who commission whichever lure best ensures their personal gain, (2) people who read or write things like this essay, and (3) people who work the floors of the casinos, clean the thousands of hotel rooms belonging to each resort, serve as cops or firemen on first-responder teams and, in general, comprise the other piece of the jig-saw puzzle that, upon completion, shows Las Vegas to be the city where America best comes into view as a land of the End in a salutary, and not just destructive, sense.

When my wife and I visited Vegas we were both struck by how startlingly free the city appeared to be from the gender confusion now reigning in other American cities. Is it because the people who serve meals and deal cards in Vegas casinos are working rather than playing games? Or because they live in North Las Vegas under Charleston Peak (11,916 ft) in the Spring Mountains? Whatever the reason, they appear to have already learned what the rest of us must now learn by laboriously working out our salvation in fear and trembling per St. Paul, St. Thomas More, and, especially, Søren Kierkegaard.

Though "fear and trembling" as a phrase shows up first in the Book of Psalms, it was St. Paul's phrasing that really established the phrase in our collective mind, owing to a powerful moment in his first epistle to Corinthians, where he asks recipients (us as well as Greeks) to "work out [our] salvation with fear and trembling" by discerning, day-to-day, what obedience (from *obedire*, to hear and maintain a sense of balance) requires. It's had a long currency, this counsel, and lest there be doubt of its staying power you have only to think of Robert Bolt's play, *A Man for All Seasons*, in which Bolt has More saying to his wife that he aspires "to serve God wittily, in the tangle of his mind."[4] Yet the version that rings best for moderns is unquestionably Kierkegaard's, partly because he devoted two whole (strikingly

3. Clarke, *The City and the Stars*, 63.

4. Bolt, *A Man for All Seasons*, 128.

readable) books to glossing the phrase but mainly because of the "either/or" concept itself. The signal book—for Kierkegaard as well as for ourselves—is (of course) *Either/Or* (published in 1843) where the protagonist, poised for a leap, trembles while standing on the brink of a very deep divide. The leap will take the protagonist from the relative safety of false choices represented by "ethical" and "aesthetic" stages of life to an unfamiliar "religious" stage whose existence is sensed but not proved. Needless to say the protagonist is going to leap, and the moral of Kierkegaard's tale is that by leaping and in that sense committing to mortal stakes the protagonist will live in the light of day, as becomes evident in *Fear and Trembling* (also published in 1843), where the so-called "knight of faith" is quite ordinary and recognizable solely by a gait that is "steady as a postman's."

Romano Guardini, for his part, thought of our intensifying need to take a stand for or against reality in almost entirely Kierkegaardian terms, and he explained the importance of those same terms as follows:

> The world to come will be filled with animosity and danger, but it will be a world open and clean. . . . The cultural deposit preserved by the Church thus far will not be able to endure against the general decay of tradition. Loneliness in faith will be terrible. . . . If we speak here of the nearness of the End, we do not mean nearness in the sense of time, but nearness as it pertains to the essence of the End, for in essence man's existence is now nearing an ultimate decision.[5]

Guardini wrote those words in 1956, right as cybernetics got a crucial boost from rocketry research occasioned by the arms race.

Did Kierkegaard know that his either/or concept would prove to be a crucial aid for generations following him?

Given the sort of books produced by Kierkegaard in later years, especially *The Present Age*, I suspect he did. How could he not, given that Tocqueville had already, just eight years before, experienced his own kind of religious fear while contemplating the safety and comfort promised to United States citizens by an "immense and tutelary power"? But regardless of what Kierkegaard's undoubtedly "indirect" answer to our question would be, we can all of us be grateful for the way in which his either/or concept enables us, for at least a few more years, to deduce an integrative center whose removal generated virtually every false opposite set entrapping us, and thereby find the courage to develop the habit of looking for

5. Guardini, *The End of the Modern World*, 105–109.

whatever window designers of our soon-to-be-realized Diaspar may unwittingly leave open. That way, when amusements have mastered every last one of us thanks to simulacra finally replacing the things they used to represent, at least one or two hopefully good souls in whom our distinctly American, backcountry-generated, PI ethos runs strong may, by chance, discover a vent like the one Arthur C. Clark's protagonist eventually finds and get *outside* to a place where entire galaxies not made by us are everywhere in view and an evening star shines brightly in the western sky. Who knows? Perhaps, out of sheer astonishment, they will instinctively recite a dimly remembered prayer. Like *Alma Redemptoris Mater*, composed in the early eleventh century.

How does it go? one of them will ask. *Quae pervia caeli, porta manes*? Yes, the other will say. Gate of heaven. Star of the sea. *Surgere qui curat populo.*

Bibliography

Bacovcin, Helen. *The Way of a Pilgrim*. New York: Image, 1992.

Beckett, Lucy. *In the Light of Christ: Writings in the Western Tradition*. San Francisco: Ignatius, 2006.

Belloc, Hilaire. *The Path to Rome*. Washington, DC: Regnery Gateway, 1987.

Bolt, Robert. *A Man for All Seasons: A Play in Two Acts*. New York: Vintage, 1980.

Chomsky, Noam. "The False Promise of Chat GPT." *New York Times* (March 8, 2023).

Clarke, Arthur C. *The City and the Stars*. London: Orion, 2001.

Delbanco, Andrew. *Melville: His Life and Work*. New York: Vintage, 2005.

Fleming, Ian. *You Only Live Twice*. London: Ian Fleming Productions, 2023.

Gibson, William. *Neuromancer*. New York: Ace Books, 1984.

Guardini, Romano. *The End of the Modern World*. Washington, DC: Regnery Gateway, 2022.

———. *Letters from Lake Como: Explorations in Technology and the Human Race*. Grand Rapids: Eerdmans, 1994.

Homer, *The Iliad*. Translated by Robert Fagles. New York: Penguin, 1990.

———. *The Odyssey*, Translated by Robert Fagles. New York: Penguin, 1996.

Johnson, Thomas H., ed. *The Complete Poems of Emily Dickinson*. Boston: Little Brown, 1960.

Kierkegaard, Søren. *Either/Or*. Translated by Swenson, David F., and Swenson, Lillian Marvin. Princeton: Princeton University Press, 1971.

———. *Fear and Trembling*. Translated by Hong, Howard V., and Hong, Edna H. Princeton: Princeton University Press, 1983.

Kissinger, Henry. *Genesis: Artificial Intelligence, Hope, and the Human Spirit*. Boston: Little Brown, 2024.

Leonard, Elmore, *The Big Bounce. New York: William Morrow, 2012.*

———. *Four Novels of the 1980s: City Primeval, La Brava, Glitz, Freaky Deaky*. New York: Library of America, 2015.

———. *Pronto*. New York: William Morrow, 2012.

———. *Rum Punch*. New York: William Morrow, 2012.

Lucas, Dave. *Weather*. Athens: University of Georgia Press, 2015.

Ludlum, Robert. *The Bourne Identity*. New York: Bantam Mass Market, 2016.

Matthiessen, Francis Otto. *American Renaissance: Art and Expression in the Age of Emerson and Whitman*. London: Oxford University Press, 1941.

McCarthy, Cormac. *Blood Meridian:The Evening Redness of the West*. New York: Vintage, 1992.

———. *The Passenger*. New York: Vintage, 2022.

———. *The Road*. New York: Vintage, 2006.

———. *Stella Maris*. London: Picador, 2022.

Melville, Herman. *Clarel: A Poem and Pilgrimage in the Holy Land*. Evanston, Illinois: Northwestern University Press, 2008.

———. *The Confidence Man: His Masquerade*. Mineola, NY: Dover, 2017.

———. *Moby Dick*. London: J.M. Dent and Sons, 1975.

Muir, John. *The Mountains of California*. Boston: Houghton Mifflin, 1894.

———. *My First Summer in the Sierra*. San Francisco: Sierra Club Books, 1988.

———. *Stories of My Boyhood and Youth*. San Francisco: Sierra Club Books, 1989.

———. *A Thousand-Mile Walk to the Gulf*. Boston: Houghton Mifflin, 1911.

Olson, Charles. *Call Me Ishmael: A Study of Melville*. San Francisco: City Lights, 1947.

Pekar, Harvey. *American Splendor*. New York: Four Walls Eight Windows, 1991.

Piiparenen, Rickey, and Trubeck, Anne, eds. *The Cleveland Anthology*. Cleveland: Belt Publishing, 2012.

Segedy, Jason, ed. *The Akron Anthology*. Cleveland: Belt Publishing, 2016.

Schjeldahl, Peter. "Insurance Man." *The New Yorker* (May 2, 2016).

Stone, Robert. *A Hall of Mirrors*. New York: Ecco, 1997.

Thompson, Hunter S. *Fear and Loathing in Las Vegas: A Savage Journey to the Heart of the American Dream*. New York: Vintage, 1998.

Thoreau, Henry David. *Kataadn*. New York: Tanam, 1980.

———. *Walden and Other Writings*. New York: Modern Library, 1950.

Tocqueville, Alexis. *Democracy in America*. Translated by Harvey C. Mansfield and Debra Winthrop. Chicago: University of Chicago Press, 2000.

Vermeule, Adrian. *Common Good Constitutionalism*. Cambridge, UK: Polity, 2022.

Virgil, *The Aeneid*. Translated by Robert Fagles. New York: Penguin, 2006.

Weaver, Richard M. *Ideas Have Consequences*. Chicago: University of Chicago Press, 1948.

Whitman, Walt. *Complete Poetry and Prose*. New York: Library of America, 1982.

Wiener, Norbert. *Cybernetics: Control and Communication in the Animal and the Machine*. Cambridge, MA: MIT Press, 1948.

Wolfe, Linnie Marsh. *Son of the Wilderness: The Life of John Muir*. New York: Knopf, 1945.

Zoffer, Josh. "Overwhelmed by the Trump Era? Try a Different Timeline." *Wall Street Journal* (December 13, 2024).

www.ingramcontent.com/pod-product-compliance
Lightning Source LLC
LaVergne TN
LVHW090526110826
845146LV00003B/998
* 9 7 9 8 3 8 5 2 6 9 7 1 6 *